Blending Temperaments

Blending Temperaments

Improving Relationships—
Yours and Others

Ruth McRoberts Ward
Rev. John E. McRoberts
Chaplain Marvin A. McRoberts

BAKER BOOK HOUSE
Grand Rapids, Michigan 49516

Scripture taken from the HOLY BIBLE, NEW INTERNATIONAL
VERSION®, copyright © 1973, 1978, 1984 International Bible Society. Used
by permission of Zondervan Bible Publishers.

Original art by Dean Vavak

Copyright © 1988 by Baker Books
a division of Baker Book House Company
P.O. Box 6287, Grand Rapids, MI 49516-6287

ISBN: 0-8010-9687-1

Fourth printing, October 1995

Printed in the United States of America

To my husband, **Jim;**
Gloria, brother John's wife;
and **Eileen,** brother Mac's wife—
who patiently put up with and
adjusted to their Intuitive
spouses' temperament "typing" language

Contents

Foreword

Alexis de Tocqueville was a brilliant nineteenth-century French journalist who wrote the classic work on the American character, *Democracy in America*. In it he noted that the survival of this country's society was dependent on its people being able to maintain a fine balance between their inclination to self-expressive individualism on the one hand, and their sense of duty to others on the other. This objective observer realized that Americans seemed to seek personal happiness and fulfillment by "doing their own thing." Americans, de Tocqueville discovered, were people who felt that they had to "be themselves" by doing those things that "turned them on" and expressed the inner longings of their souls. The journalist suspected that these strong tendencies toward self-actualization and ego gratification could eventually lead the American people to massive self-destruction unless they were held in check by an equally strong sense of personal obligation to the well-being of others. He believed that the necessary balance to the self-expressiveness of Americans was provided by a deep sense of duty, which stemmed from the teachings they received through their families and churches. As long as families and churches inspired people to put others before themselves, de Tocqueville believed, Americans would be able to check these self-cen-

9

tered tendencies, which otherwise would make them into neurotic narcissists.

If de Tocqueville could visit the America of today, he would be dismayed to see that what he had hoped would not happen has come to pass in ways that have exceeded his imagination. Americans have become a people seemingly bent on unchecked self-actualization. Many of us have fallen in love with "human potential" courses that promise we can become our best selves by going after what we want. We have adopted the pop ideology of "Jonathan Livingston Seagull" and believe we can be fully alive only if we have the courage to break out of the constraints imposed on us by the expectations of others.

What has gone wrong in America is that the institutions meant to check and balance our emphasis on self-expression and personal fulfillment have themselves become propagators of narcissism. Even marriage, which was once an arrangement in which we committed ourselves to serve each other in mutual love, has come to be viewed as a relationship that exists only to help individuals gratify their personal hunger for happiness. (Consequently, when we find that our marriages are unfulfilling, we try to get out of them.) We have little sense of obligation to others and seem to care only for our own gratification. With "duty be damned" as our motto, we say to ourselves, "I owe it to myself to be happy, no matter what it costs or who gets hurt!" In marriage, the idea of staying together "till death us do part" has become for too many people an old-fashioned, self-limiting concept. A modern bride or groom might rewrite the marital vows to read "I promise to stay with you till I no longer find this relationship capable of meeting *my* psychic and emotional needs."

Churches, too, seem to have lost the capacity to foster a sense of loyalty and responsibility in their members. Many people want no part of religious institutions that press them to be dutiful. They prefer churches that meet their individual needs. Consequently, some worship services have become merely group-therapy sessions for the bourgeoisie. Pentecostal churches are not much better than those in the mainstream of Christendom. Our charismatic brothers and sisters, too, often articulate theologies of prosperity that promise economic well-being and happiness in this life in addition to pie-in-the-sky when we die.

We want to silence all that talk about suffering children in the Third World or people living under oppressive political regimes propped up by U.S. dollars—even though we know that Jesus calls us to feed the hungry, to bring deliverance to captive peoples, and to commit ourselves to taking up the cross to follow him. How much more pleasant to hear about a God who will give us a new Cadillac in our favorite color if we will just get into praying for it "in his name"! What most people seem to want is a religion that makes a personal emotional "turn on" the ultimate *raison d'etre*. Despite Jesus' call that we sacrifice all for his sake and for the sake of others, self-denial no longer has a place in our new religious fervor.

In Robert Bellah's new book, *Habits of the Heart,* the author points out that there is at least one group of people who stand against this overemphasis on self-expressiveness: evangelical Christians. Bellah finds that the evangelicals' strong adherence to the teachings of the Bible has led them to feel called to fulfill God-ordained duties to others. These Christians believe they must stay in marriages simply because God commands them to do so. Furthermore, each partner is obligated to make the happiness of the spouse more important than his or her own. Evangelicals believe that their churches should be made up of believers more committed to serving the needs of others than seeking to have their own needs served. In what must be viewed as a strange claim to the rest of the world, they say, "Only those who give away their lives in duty to others in the name of Christ will ever know the fullness of life."

This book is about the evangelical perspectives on personal relationships. Its authors endeavor to show us how to find joy by working out the meaning of commitment to Christ in our everyday interactions with others. The book lays out some of the profound insights of the simple gospel message. It declares that obedience to what God calls us to do and be is the basis of "abundant living."

As the authors share with us experiences from their own lives, they help us to see what life in Christ can be like. They try to show us how we can have positive self-images without narcissism and to lead us into the sense of dignity and worth that comes from being on a mission from God. Finally, they do their best to explain how we can live out our lives joyfully and constructively in relationship to others, all in the name of Christ.

Books like this one are necessary because they buck the destructive trend toward unrestrained self-centeredness everywhere evident in America today. This book speaks to us in easy-to-understand ways about how we can make our lives work for good.

But enough of my sociological ramblings. It is time you get on with reading a book that I believe can make a big difference in your life.

Tony Campolo
Professor of Sociology
Eastern College

Preface

The ideas presented here stem, for the most part, from my day-to-day counseling sessions and from the family-enrichment conferences that my husband, Jim, and I conduct. (Since confidentiality is essential, names and situations have been altered to preserve the anonymity of my clients.)

I hear daily such things as "I just can't live up to his expectations" or "I've done everything I can think of and she still doesn't approve of me." Another common theme is "I would like to tell people how I feel, but I wouldn't want to hurt their feelings or make them angry." Similarly, "Why is it that I say yes, when I mean no? I resent the person who asked me, yet I feel guilty if I don't comply."

Most people, regardless of their age, want to be respected for who they are and appreciated for what they do. However, when how we act or speak does not match others' expectations, we may experience feelings of inadequacy, anger, and guilt, which spawn resentments and bitterness. Unresolved anger and stored resentment often seed depression and other illnesses. These emotional upheavals block good communication and destroy creativity.

Ironically, most guilt-producing expectations are either unfair, unspoken, unrealistic, childish, or selfish. Careful examination of our guilt relieves and releases, giving new confidence. Ideally, expressions of anger assist in identifying the sources of our guilt feelings. When understood, appreciated, and rightly used, anger becomes a friend rather than a foe.

Understanding God's different patterns of temperament is the key to blending expectations, ultimately producing and/or improving communication, which in turn eases tensions and dissolves unnecessary guilt.

Blending Temperaments will pinpoint analogies between various personality types and flower species in a garden. Even though each variety of flower possesses unique qualities, all plants have similar needs and face common problems as they work together to achieve a clean garden. They struggle against pesky insects, compete with greedy weeds, deal with a lack of water, resist destructive winds and foul weather, and submit to necessary pruning.

Accepting yourself as God designed you is the road to healthy self-esteem. Understanding and accepting the way God designed others is the marked path to unity and harmony. The sooner we understand spiritual gifting, the sooner we will walk according to God's plan.

This book will offer guidelines for nurturing relationships with your children, spouses, co-workers, and fellow believers. Many of these suggestions parallel the ways one would cultivate a garden with careful, skillful, daily attention.

Since the condition of home and family is critical, two chapters have been contributed by two of my brothers from their gleanings as pastoral marriage counselors. This material is well-suited for either marriage enrichment or premarital counseling.

Ruth Ward
York, Pennsylvania

Acknowledgments

I would like especially to thank Jim for his total support as chief critic, advisor, and encourager. As well as being a sounding board, my friend Lynne Strayer shared gardening tips and helped me match temperaments with appropriate flowers. I am also indebted to our daughter, Kay Baldwin, and to several friends—too many to list—who listened, offered suggestions, and critiqued chapters. Naturally, I am grateful to the clients who gave me permission to share their ideas and growth in understanding.

John wishes to thank his wife, Gloria, and his office staff: Sherry Heath, Sherry Calendine, and Susan Hopkins.

Mac also thanks his wife, Eileen—Gloria's sister—for her support and encouragement.

All three of us are indebted to our mother and the rest of our extended family for their interest and encouragement and our clients for their willingness to trust our counsel.

1

Self-Esteem—
Recognizing Our
Differences

Let us therefore make every effort to do what leads to peace and to mutual edification. Romans 14:19

A healthy self-image is the ticket to open, honest communication and harmony—what most human beings are really thirsting for. The camouflaged resentment that springs out of all kinds of unfulfilled expectations fuels subtle fires of low self-esteem at every level.

Most of us have known for years that low self-esteem can be a serious burden for individuals, but now even the Gallup Poll has declared that it is the number-one problem in American society. Obviously, we need help in understanding ourselves and others in order to improve our quality of life.

Boy, Are We Ever Different!

Men, do you ever wonder why some fellows have little interest in taking care of simple maintenance on their automobiles and procrastinate making small repairs around the house, even though they know how?

Ladies, do you wonder why your sister enjoys doing handicrafts and your friend delights in house cleaning, while neither activity interests you much? Or, whatever your gender, do you ever wonder why some people rarely speak up and others never keep quiet?

Moms, do you ever wonder why your teenage daughter keeps a messy room, though you've trained her to do better? And why is that same offspring or her brother sometimes stubborn as a mule, resisting your lists and helpful suggestions?

Teachers, ever wonder why some students are assertive and self-confident while others resist leadership and dialogue—even kids from the same home? Or why some students possess self-discipline in turning in papers and others struggle with meeting deadlines?

Wives or husbands, do you ever wonder why your spouse bends over backwards to aid relatives or people at work yet resists your simple requests for help? Or are you puzzled about why he or she hates to crawl out of bed in the

morning, resists turning in at night, and dislikes setting an alarm, punching a time clock, or being put on a schedule? Or why your mate withholds details of the workday or "people news" unless the subject comes up?

Kids, do you ever wonder why your parents insist on knowing your destination, companions, and returning time?

Why are some people so casual about completing projects—yet others can't rest until they finish?

Why do some people find it difficult to say "I'm sorry" or "I was wrong"? And why do some men assume their decisions are sounder than females'?

Isn't it strange, also, that some people give the impression that they know it all and seem to question everything you say?

Take heart, any of you who have wondered about such things! Most people do not really intend to be uncaring, unfriendly, offensive, or arrogant. They just come across that way because of their characteristic style of dealing with the world.

The majority of "strange" behavioral responses can be explained by the different ways individuals prefer to gather information and make decisions, their social orientation toward either extraversion or introversion, and their choice between structured or spontaneous lifestyles. Since all our basic traits are unique gifts from our Creator, knowing one's God-designed temperament removes the need to apologize for how one prefers to think and act and produces patience toward others who prefer to think and act in opposite ways.

For some odd reason, we often find ourselves surrounded by people who think and behave differently from us—even our biological children or natural parents. The normal reaction is to label another's unusual or unexpected ideas and behavior as insecurities, immaturities, inferiorities, arrogance, weakness, laziness, snobbishness or selfishness, all of which negative terms imply that the other person has upset our level of expectations.

God created us as creatures of communication and growth. He wants us to use and improve our ease and enjoyment of assisting ourselves and others in maintaining healthy relationships with him, as well as with those with whom we rub shoulders at home, work, church, club, and school.

It behooves us, therefore, to acquaint ourselves with the God-designed temperament differences, not only to help us cope with others but, more importantly, to avoid resentments and blend our expectations with theirs.

My book *Self-Esteem—Gift from God* describes and discusses the various temperaments, showing how understanding innate preferences raises individual self-esteem, promotes appreciation of others, and improves communication in every dimension of life.

To assist clients and seminar attenders in determining their personal temperament type, I use the Myers-Briggs Temperament Indicator (MBTI)—a highly researched yet simple personal survey developed by a lay person, Katharine C. Briggs, and her daughter, Isabel Myers, and drawn from C. G. Jung's ideas on psychological type.

This type of study is guaranteed to nurture your self-esteem, and at the same time considerably improve your communication skills. As a bonus, it will provide a candid, fresh, and flattering portrait of your spouse, co-workers, children, and acquaintances—anyone who crosses your lifestyle. You will not only find personal relief but will be able to encourage others more effectively.

How We Are Different

The following outline combines a shortened version of the interpretation of the MBTI that I give my clients with gleanings from self-esteem seminar workshops. It should help you pinpoint your own preferences in each of four major dimensions that blend together to make up one's temperament: social preference, information gathering, decision making, and lifestyle.

Social Preference: Inner and Outer Worlds

Privacy-Prone Introverts

God has designed about 25 percent of the world to be decidedly turned inward, having a high preference for privacy rather than people, and peace and quiet rather than noise and confusion. The remainder of the population is Extraverted to some degree, possessing a greater capacity for crowds, noise, and confusion and a lower need for privacy. The world in general seems more receptive to Extraverts, which often puts their opposites at a distinct disadvantage.

"When my wife's feet hit the floor in the morning," an Introvert shared, "her tongue is activated. Or is it tongues?" he quipped. Some Introverts cleverly stay in bed until their Extravert spouse has cleared out, so they can dress and breakfast in silence.

Introverts avoid crowded gatherings, preferring one-on-one relationships. They usually do not choose to converse unless they are comfortable and the group is small, while most Extraverts have little problem engaging strangers in conversation or speaking up in large gatherings.

Introverts generally weigh words and ponder before they speak—"mind editing," I call it—which reduces verbal blunders, but produces slower responses. "By the time I sift and decide what I want to say," one businessman Introvert complained, "someone else has either verbalized what I intended to say or has moved on to another subject. Frustrating. I just listen."

"Not having the opportunity to put our two cents in," a quality-control man defended, "we Introverts are thought to be dull, bored, mad, or sad. Or worse yet, stuck up. We're usually none of those," he continued. "We have plenty to say if people would just give us opportunity."

Many Introverts agree that people often ask them if everything is okay. Without realizing it, an Introvert's silence and sobriety—often misinterpreted as confidence and knowledge—can be intimidating to an Extravert. A familiar proverb says, "Even a fool is thought wise if he keeps silent . . ." (Prov. 17:28).

It often amazes Introverts to learn that others are frightened of them. "People have no idea how I shudder inside," a successful businessman shared. "I'm never completely comfortable giving reports to large groups."

"We fear someone is going to ask a question we can't or don't want to answer," a small group of Introverts shared. "We prefer to have plenty of time to think about our answer because we like our information to be not only pertinent but accurate as well."

Because Introverts are thorough contemplators, their observations and statements are often profound. Many Extraverts find this ability very attractive. But, since Introverts prefer to keep personal problems, feelings, and opinions to themselves, only those who have won their trust know them well.

Because Introverts have a tendency to bottle up their anger and other emotions, they suffer more often with depression. Their careful calculations can result in pessimism. Although Introverts seem to be stoic, they are usually quite sensitive, feel hurts and slights, and care deeply for others.

People-Prone Extraverts

Extraverts generally speak first, then think, and then perhaps adjust what they just said. They absorb energies from other people and carry erasers. Extraverts rely on what I call "ear editing."

"I really don't know what I'm thinking until I hear myself talk," many Extraverts confess. "I talk until I think of something to say," Garrison Keillor, a popular monologist and author quips.

Since Introverts test statements before they ever leave their brains, their misstatements remain unspoken. Extraverts, for the most part, test their statements by ear as well as the looks on listeners' faces. Extraverts readily voice their opinions, volunteering how they feel, how much weight they've lost or gained, or what's happened so far today, and openly discuss projects they are working on. Many Extraverts admit that they are amazed at what and how much they say. In fact, Extraverts are often attracted to Introverts just because they are good listeners.

"It seems like you Extraverts are afraid of no one and never at a loss for words," a workshop group of Introverts concluded. "We really envy those abilities."

"Even though we may exude a fearless, self-confident impression," an Extravert replied, "we do get nervous and bandy-legged at times. We just don't let on."

However, Extraverts' optimism, self-confidence, and ability not to take themselves or setbacks too seriously greatly redeem their wordiness. "Extraverts keep us Introverts from being so boring," a small group of the latter observed. "They also are good at easing awkward situations with their humorous banter."

Extraverts feel obligated to fill the airwaves because they assume that lulls in conversation are just as annoying to others as to them. Not so. An Extravert's tendency to finish a slow speaker's sentences (because he or she prefers immediate responses and also has something more to say) irritates both Introverts and other less confident or stammering Extraverts. "Extraverts almost choke on what they know," a workshop member shared.

Because, by God's design, Extraverts require exposure to many people and little privacy, being alone is as distasteful to some of them as being with too many people is to Introverts. Some simply must have conversation and/or people around them most of the day or they become restless or suffer from boredom and depression. Usually these feelings last only until they get around people again.

Extraverts can and must learn to edit their voluminous verbiage, if not for others' benefit, then—for their own protection—to trim away the need for "I spoke out of turn" statements. I often suggest cutting what they want to say in half as a practical goal. Learning to listen is a skill worth cultivating.

On the other hand, if Introverts would smile a bit more and risk jumping into conversations by announcing that "I have something to say," they would destroy some of Extraverts' wrong assumptions about them and will bless the world with their unique humor, opinions, and ideas.

The most distinguishing contrast between introversion and extraversion is the effect people have on them. Being with people drains Introverts but charges up Extraverts. The biggest favor that Extraverts can bestow on Introverts is to grant them privacy and recouping time—while Introverts should learn to inform Extraverts when their ears are weary.

Neither way of reacting to the outer world is superior. Most normal people are a blend of both introversion and extraversion. To be totally extraverted or introverted might indicate serious emotional or social problems.

Gathering Information: Facts vs. Ideas

Two processes used simultaneously influence life's direction—information gathering and decision making. (The latter will be discussed separately.) The two main sources for information gathering are our *senses* and *intuition*. Our sensory systems collect and catalog black-and-white facts and figures that aid survival in the conscious world. Intuition supplies abstract ideas and possibilities that are especially helpful in problem solving and design. For good balance, we need to rely on both our senses and our intuitive abilities and *blend* the information gathered from each. Most people do just that, but—on an individual basis—one source is easier and more appealing to use, while the other requires a disciplined effort.

"Feet on the Ground"

Those who strongly prefer sensory information gathering—75 percent of the nation—discover that their "observers are always on." They automatically pick up physical data with their eyes, ears, nose, touch, and tongue. Cataloguing physical facts, figures, dates and details comes naturally. Such people pride themselves on being accurate and exact and are perplexed when others forget the things they can remember so easily. In arguments, Sensing people can destroy Intuitives with facts and are sometimes characterized as having a feet-on-the-ground approach to life.

Those who prefer to learn through their senses, are generally attracted to hands-on careers and involvements. Once they master a product, service, or technique, they enjoy repeating the process, which results in perfection, high production, and growth. Their tolerance for repetition keeps them from being bored and gives them a healthy capacity for routine. "Routine is necessary to make the world go round," a Sensing seminar group agreed. "We earn tenure awards because we stick with what we like," one member added.

"I like to know what is expected of me and appreciate having all the supplies that I need on hand," another shared. "For people like us, what we are working on is what we are thinking about. That's why we make fewer mistakes. We are proud of what we accomplish."

"We like our ability to use common sense and to follow directions as well as rules. Why have rules if you're not going to follow them?" is the reasoning for sense-oriented individuals. "We dislike radical change, preferring the simplicity of gradual adjustments. Please give us plenty of time to digest facts before pressing for decisions. We aren't slow or dull. We're just more accurate."

The rest of the world sometimes takes for granted Sensing people's contributions toward keeping things comfortable, solvent, beautiful, and moving smoothly. This group is conscious of today, yet aware of yesterday. They automatically check with past experience before making decisions. That explains some of their reluctance to "try it again."

"We like to keep life simple," the Sensing group explained. "One thing at a time," "Don't fix it if it isn't broken," and "We've always done it this way" are statements that could describe their general approach.

The world is greatly indebted to the many Sensing people who faithfully serve as bankers, doctors, nurses, mechanics, bookkeepers, administrators, secretaries, teachers, factory workers, salespersons, and dozens of other product-related service careers. However, many of these people have also found their way into Intuitive careers and responsibilities and have contributed significantly. The Intuitive world needs their steady hands and physical decisions, as we will see below.

"Head in the Clouds"

People who prefer the Intuitive way of gathering information are more alive to the unknown world of possibility thinking, design, hunches, and "what might be." Their constant jumble of ideas seems to leave little room or time for facts, figures, and practical concerns. Perhaps the stereotypical "absent-minded professor" best typifies this head-in-the-clouds approach.

"If we lose our date books or brief cases, we're in big trouble," one Intuitive shared with his group. "We remember the facts that we think are important or will support our case, but we prefer to find solutions through our possibility thinking."

Because Intuitives prefer using mental processes, they

are often impatient with performing repetitious physical activities. For example, they may find the routine of cutting grass, auto and home maintenance, housework, bookkeeping, and the like not only boring but unfulfilling.

Intuitives are usually surprised to learn that their incessant questions may intimidate a Senser, especially one who assumes that interrogators are smart. "Maybe he's after my job," a Sensing person worries, not realizing that curiosity, and an insatiable hunger to learn new things, prompts an Intuitive to probe for subtle information.

Whereas Sensing people like to produce a useful product, system, or service, Intuitives prefer to improve the same. However, once they learn the ropes, unless there's lots of variety and change, they often lose interest and crave new goals and challenges.

The goal of Intuitives is to *have* a goal. They want to be involved in projects that are bigger than themselves. If nothing is left to master, their interest wanes. This explains why some people have had many unrelated jobs or earned several degrees by the time they reach retirement years.

"We admit that we're 'Jack of all trades and masters of none,'" an Intuitive shared with the group. "We'd really like to display one thing that we do well. But Alas! who can see inside our minds?" These people prefer that each day be "different" in order to break routine, still another reason why time-clock jobs are distasteful to them. Many create mind games in order to neutralize the boredom.

Because Intuitives have the ability to see all around and beyond an event—maybe ten years or more down the road—they may come across as preoccupied, flaky or distant. Or they may "chase many rabbits" in meetings. But these people have to learn to cut off their ideas and get to decision time. It's true that "the lights are on but nobody's home" certainly describes Intuitives at times. "But, honestly, we *are* busy in there," an Intuitive explained.

"Looking beyond the present situation of details—seeing

the big picture—appeals to us," one Intuitive explained to his group. "We admit that we spend too much time in indecision or going in circles, where we miss a lot of what's going on. But what's going to happen tomorrow is much more exciting to us than what's going on right now. We prefer to prevent problems. Appreciate us for our ideas and we'll be happy."

Although Intuitives are known to stir the pot, the world is indebted to them for systems analyses, counseling, writing, research, pastoring, and other careers that involve theory, behavior, and improving mental and emotional health. The Sensing world is richer for having a few Intuitives who dream and are not afraid to make radical changes for improvement.

Remember, everyone is a blend of both the sensing and intuitive preferences, leaning more one way than the other. However, each must consult and use both preferences as situations demand.

Decision Making: Logic vs. Emotions

Two considerations—head and heart—influence our decision making and determine the method we will use in most situations. Logical, "head" decisions based on cold facts are Thinking-oriented. Emotional, "heart" decisions involving people and values indicate a Feeling preference.

For overall social development and stability, a person needs occasionally to exercise and blend both methods of decision making. But again, by God's design, each individual tends to trust and depend on one method more than the other and find it easier and more natural to use. Some people think first with the head; others think first with the heart. Learning to consult the opposite option requires time, discipline, and daily practice.

"Do What's Sensible"

People who prefer using the Thinking method are often regarded as cold, inconsiderate, stubborn, selfish, impatient, unforgiving, or all-business. They rarely admit their decisions are wrong unless irrefutable facts prove them so.

"Logical" people seem to get their own way by addressing the immediate issue. Because they are not driven to please others and maintain harmony, they consider only what seems most practical and fair, economical, or efficient, rather than how others might feel about it. Those who think with their heads make a decision and expect approval whereas those who think with their hearts prefer to get approval before making a decision.

Thinkers base their decisions on cause-and-effect practicalities, preferring to make situation-based choices. They trust their own decisions most and want others to respect their judgment powers and admire them afterwards.

Thinkers must learn that logical decisions are not always the best ones, that sometimes relationships with other people are more important than anything else. Those who rely heavily on what their head tells them are capable of making impersonal, unpopular, distasteful, and disappointing decisions that their Feeling opposites dislike and avoid. Granted, tough, logical decisions keep the world upright, rational, and stable. Although Feeling people are often intimidated and even frightened by Thinkers, they are indebted to them for security.

"We do not make decisions out of spite or intentionally to take advantage of others' weakness," a Thinking workshop group defended. "We just prefer to make sensible decisions that conserve time, money, and energy. Sure, we respect peace and harmony, but we can function without them."

Many Thinking people affirm that it demands real effort to be alert to others' need for praise and appreciation, to be sensitive to the silent expectations for attention and affection that others likely place on them. "Thinking people don't seem to have any emotions," a Feeling group observed. "They are always controlled."

"We *do* have feelings," a Thinking group countered. "We

just don't allow emotions to control the decision. Our hurts usually don't linger, because we think through the whole situation and forget it. But we do need help in acknowledging and understanding our feelings."

The complaint often leveled at Thinkers is their reluctance to pass on news they consider irrelevant to the situation. "My husband never shares anything about work," one wife said. "I learn more from a secondhand phone conversation." When confronted with his negligence in this respect, the husband calmly replied: "When I spend eight to ten hours in the jungle of jangled nerves, do you think I want to come home and go over all of it again, and load you up with all that garbage, too? I consider my family a separate priority and refuse to let my career consume my attention when I'm home."

Thinkers have a tendency to store information for later reference, drawing upon it only if the subject related to those facts surfaces. (On the other hand, Feeling people voluntarily transfer such tidbits as "Guess what I heard today!" to anyone they feel would be interested.) Therefore, Thinkers' friends and family are often incensed and hurt to be the last to learn pertinent data since the Feeling segment of one's personhood measures its importance by the amount of information received from a loved one. Thinkers can develop a sharing attitude by making notes throughout the day of events and news that they think their "softhearted" counterparts would find interesting.

It has been reliably documented and psychologists agree that 60 percent of men and 40 percent of women prefer Thinking decision making. The special problems of logic-oriented women will be covered in a later chapter.

"Do What Feels Comfortable"

Fifty percent of the nation find thinking with the heart decisions more natural than using pure logic. Emotional decision-makers are strongly influenced by their own and other peoples' needs and opinions. Being in agreement, getting others' approval, and sidestepping arguments appeals to Feeling deciders more than just saving money, time, or energy. They avoid confrontations because they dislike criticism of themselves—a weakness that needs to be faced.

A significant characteristic of Feeling people is their preference for making choices that benefit others. Careers or jobs that directly affect the lives of others, such as sales, social work, and service attract many Feeling people.

Before Feeling people make a decision, they consider how others will receive it. For example, "I know you counted on my being home this evening, but I have to work late. I'm very sorry." A Thinker would more likely say, "I won't be home for dinner." Period!

Feeling people are naturally apologetic and hate to hurt feelings. They are skilled at giftwrapping or explaining their statements: "Your dessert looks scrumptious, but if you don't mind, I'll pass on it this time. I'm counting calories." Or they may preface their opinions with such conciliatory remarks as "You may disagree with me, but. . . ." They generally choose the flexible word *feel* rather than the decisive word *think*.

Although they dislike disagreements and fights, Feelers are most often the ones involved in scraps, because their sensitive emotions easily erupt over hurt feelings, rejections, and slights. Many cry easily in response to either good or bad news. Feeling deciders want everyone to like them, even those they dislike. Since maintaining peace is their common goal, they have difficulty living or working without harmony.

"We want to know that we are liked, and have others' acceptance and approval," one Feeler explained in a seminar. "We want to feel like we are part of a group and fit. If someone doesn't want us around, we prefer to leave."

Because they don't want to disappoint anyone, Feeling people do many things they don't want to do—saying "yes" when they mean "no." They treat others as they would

like to be treated and expect others to return the favor
since they often allow others to take advantage of their
generosity of time, money, and energy. They are likely to
get angry when their gifts or favors are overlooked or
unappreciated.

Feeling deciders constantly battle mixed emotions.
Making decisions based on logic presents a difficult assignment for them.

One group of emotion-oriented decision-makers summarized their approach:

> We want the world to know that we can and do make
> many difficult decisions and that we dislike being thought
> of as wishy-washy, spineless, indecisive, and a soft touch.
> With practice, we learn to look at facts as well as our
> feelings and resist taking the blame for everything that
> goes wrong. We want to be appreciated when we go out
> of our way for people, and we like our gifts and labors of
> love to be acknowledged and appreciated. For some reason
> we thrive on praise and approval and need encouragement
> and thanks, even for doing jobs that we are getting paid
> for. We have to know that we are doing things right and
> are pleasing our superiors.

When others do not reciprocate, many Feeling people
are overcome with jealousy, self-pity, anger, or resentment.
Because they are people-oriented, Feeling deciders are
likely to put high demands on others and then suffer
emotional hurt when their expectations are ignored or
unfulfilled. Naturally, all their demands are not
reasonable.

Just as Thinkers can benefit from understanding the
Feeling deciders' perspective, so can the latter benefit from
talking with Thinkers before making final decisions.

The world is indebted to Feeling people for insisting on
and fighting for peace and harmony. They are often the
ones who give a person "one more chance," cold facts
notwithstanding.

Feelers are not saints anymore than Thinkers are sinners, as chapters 2 to 11 clarify.

As with most contrasting temperaments, the world is split fifty/fifty on Thinking and Feeling preferences. As previously stated, 60 percent of women and 40 percent of men prefer Feeling decision making. The special problems of Feeling men will be discussed in a later chapter.

Everyone blends both Feeling and Thinking in varying proportions. Home background and experiences greatly influence one's innate decision-making preference.

Lifestyle: Structure vs. Spontaneity

Differences in lifestyle preferences present a basic source of marital problems and can explain much of the friction between any two people who share a relationship, including parent and child, close friends, or worker and his or her superior. When the two lifestyle preferences reflected by God's special design are understood, they not only make good sense and ease much tension, but the differences are often a source of amusement. One couple who had been trying to change each other for years now just shrugs a shoulder and laughs about differences that once were a cause of discord. Of course, each of us is a neat combination of Structure and Spontaneity, depending not only on our inborn temperament but on background, environment, and other influences.

"Keep on Schedule"

People who prefer a Structured or organized lifestyle are work-oriented. They like to get necessary projects finished before they play. In fact, they cannot enjoy leisure unless their work is complete, though they need to learn that play is an important part of mental and physical health.

Structured people usually make lists and enjoy crossing off the items as they are polished off. They often judge the success of their day by how much was accomplished. "Work, it must be done" is their motto. "Let's get started so we can get it over with" is a favorite directive for Structured and organized people. They actually like to work, but almost everything they do is regarded as "work"—jobs they like and those they dislike. Quite often, they tackle distasteful jobs first.

Appointments and scheduling give Structured people the organized outline needed for their lives. Without a planned agenda, they may feel quite insecure. In fact, Structured people are likely to waste a day that has not been planned, though they hate themselves, afterwards. What they often forget is that everyone needs a certain amount of throwaway time to avoid burnout.

"We don't mind Structured people doing their thing," a Spontaneous seminar participant shared, "but we dislike it when they try to organize us. The group laughed when he added, "We have a different strategy of getting things done."

Typical was a remark overheard at a family campout: "We have a free day. Let's schedule it."

"Why ruin a perfectly beautiful day like that?" a Spontaneous companion retorted.

Since meeting deadlines is a serious matter to Structured people, much stress in their lives stems from the fear that they might be late. If they can hack it, they prefer to hand in papers and reports early "to play safe." Also, they bank on free time at the end (although they will most likely end up using it "productively").

"Sometimes, we hurry to finish projects and jobs only to discover later that the assignment or order has been cancelled," a Structured group member admitted. "The Spontaneous workers kind of smirk at us when that happens."

People who prefer a Structured world divide the day into segments and live by the clock. They are likely to designate certain days for specific jobs. "We have to learn to be flexible," one Structured individual admitted, "because we let our schedule and plans become law and get bent out of shape over it. Sometimes we are our worst enemies!"

"I used to really respect you people for your organization, but you can't help it," a Spontaneous observer teased.

Some Structured people give the impression that being organized is synonymous with being spiritually and emotionally mature, as though they taught themselves to be that way. Naturally, a certain degree of self-discipline results from an inner determination to control one's will and inclinations—but many highly disciplined and motivated people take the total credit for their preference for Structure and getting things done without realizing that it stems mostly from special gifting.

Time-management speakers and proponents of "setting priorities" (including preachers, parents, and teachers) decry the Spontaneous, unstructured lifestyle as though it were inferior. This condescending attitude does intimidate Spontaneous people, who have to struggle in a Structured world as it is.

God didn't goof when he created fifty percent of the world to be more Structured than the other half. He knew that Structured people would need Spontaneous counterparts to balance their tendency for workaholism.

"Follow Your Impulse"

Spontaneous people have been gifted by God with a play ethic. "Work, it must be fun" is their motto, qualified by "I'll do it later!"

Because Spontaneous people dislike being told what to do themselves, neither receiving nor giving orders is one of their natural characteristics. "Independent" and "stubborn" describe most of them to some degree. These people do not like to be boxed in. Planning their day or following a prescribed schedule does not appeal to them.

"I like to do things when I first think of it, rather than plan ahead," one Spontaneous individual said to the group. "It ruins half the fun if you have to wait for something to happen," another member continued. "What you plan to do Friday may not materialize, so you avoid disappointment by not planning. Also, appointments made way ahead may conflict with an opportunity to go to the beach," someone else expounded.

Unstructured people are process- rather than completion or closure-oriented. As long as they are challenged by what they are doing, they will continue. That explains why they prefer short-term, exciting projects. If jobs or responsibilities do not provide much stimulation, they will begin reluctantly and possibly not finish what they started. But their discipline and commitment far outshine Structured peoples' if they are sufficiently challenged.

"We do not work from lists," one Spontaneous group member reminded the others. "We hate lists and lose lists and wish our parents had understood that. We prefer to let little jobs pile up into one huge challenge. We'll do a better job cleaning if we are working on a disaster area. Please don't tell us when to begin, just when the job has to be finished" was the consensus.

God has gifted Spontaneous people to be good in an emergency or crisis. They think clearly and do their best work when they are under time pressure. In fact, they become structured in a crisis. That is why they are likely to let things slide until the last minute and then "steam it out"—and get an A on the project, whatever it is.

Since life normally consists of more routine than crisis, unless Spontaneous people have trouble-shooting professions, their best potential will go untapped. In their spare time, they may follow emergency vehicles or be involved in a sport or recreation that provides some risk factor.

When one Structured group faulted Spontaneous people for chronic tardiness, the latter countered with "We're not habitually late because of lack of respect for the people involved, but because we hate to wait for things to begin. Most meetings, for example, are pretty boring to us. We'd rather be outside. The first part of meetings is usually spent getting ready to begin, anyway."

A senior engineering student in the Spontaneous group said, "If I get up early, I get to school late, but if I sleep until the last minute, I get everything done—essential things, that is—and still make it to class on time. If I get up early, I piddle away the time reading the paper and playing with the cat."

Since the business world is organized and considers respect for the clock and dependability critical criteria for good workmanship, many Spontaneous people lose good jobs due to their poor punctuality and absenteeism. "We do not have the rigid sense of time that Structured people seem to possess," one group member responded. When a Structured person says, 'Meet me at ten,' that doesn't mean *exactly* at ten to us, but somewhere around there. We do agree, though, that improving our punctuality and dependability should be one of our chief goals. We usually accept the challenge, even though it's not much fun."

Since most Spontaneous people are obligated to work in the Structured world, they should allow themselves to be more Spontaneous after hours and on vacation. More rigidly scheduled people should learn flexibility and the subtle wisdom of playtime from their Spontaneous opposites.

What Temperament Type Are You?

To determine your temperament code letters, use the following guide. Circle your preference in each of the four categories listed below:

E *Extraversion*	Social Preference	**I** *Introversion*
S *Sensing*	Information Gathering	**N** *Intuitive*
T *Thinking*	Decision Making	**F** *Feeling*
J *Structured*	Lifestyle	**P** *Spontaneous*

The next chapters will refer often to temperament types by using the four letters. For your convenience, the Myers-

SENSING TYPES

INTROVERTS	ISTJ	ISFJ
	Serious, quiet, earn success by concentration and thoroughness. Practical, orderly, matter-of-fact, logical, realistic and dependable. See to it that everything is well organized. Take responsibility. Make up their own minds as to what should be accomplished and work toward it steadily, regardless of protests or distractions.	Quiet, friendly, responsible and conscientious. Work devotedly to meet their obligations and serve their friends and school. Thorough, painstaking, accurate. May need time to master technical subjects, as their interests are usually not technical. Patient with detail and routine. Loyal, considerate, concerned with how other people feel.
	ISTP	**ISFP**
	Cool onlookers—quiet, reserved, observing and analyzing life with detached curiosity and unexpected flashes of original humor. Usually interested in impersonal principles, cause and effect, how and why mechanical things work. Exert themselves no more than they think necessary, because any waste of energy would be inefficient.	Retiring, quietly friendly, sensitive, kind, modest about their abilities. Shun disagreements, do not force their opinions or values on others. Usually do not care to lead but are often loyal followers. Often relaxed about getting things done, because they enjoy the present moment and do not want to spoil it by undue haste or exertion.
EXTROVERTS	**ESTP**	**ESFP**
	Matter-of-fact, do not worry or hurry, enjoy whatever comes along. Tend to like mechanical things and sports, with friends on the side. May be a bit blunt or insensitive. Can do math or science when they see the need. Dislike long explanations. Are best with real things that can be worked, handled, taken apart or put together.	Outgoing, easygoing, accepting, friendly, enjoy everything and make things more fun for others by their enjoyment. Like sports and making things. Know what's going on and join in eagerly. Find remembering facts easier than mastering theories. Are best in situations that need sound common sense and practical ability with people as well as with things.
	ESTJ	**ESFJ**
	Practical, realistic, matter-of-fact, with a natural head for business or mechanics. Not interested in subjects they see no use for, but can apply themselves when necessary. Like to organize and run activities. May make good administrators, especially if they remember to consider others' feelings and points of view.	Warm-hearted, talkative, popular, conscientious, born cooperators, active committee members. Need harmony and may be good at creating it. Always doing something nice for someone. Work best with encouragement and praise. Little interest in abstract thinking or technical subjects. Main interest is in things that directly and visibly affect people's lives.

INTUITIVE TYPES

I N F J

Succeed by perseverance, originality and desire to do whatever is needed or wanted. Put their best efforts into their work. Quietly forceful, conscientious, concerned for others. Respected for their firm principles. Likely to be honored and followed for their clear convictions as to how best to serve the common good.

I N T J

Usually have original minds and great drive for their own ideas and purposes. In fields that appeal to them, they have a fine power to organize a job and carry it through with or without help. Skeptical, critical, independent, determined, often stubborn. Must learn to yield less important points in order to win the most important.

I N F P

Full of enthusiasms and loyalties, but seldom talk of these until they know you well. Care about learning, ideas, language, and independent projects of their own. Tend to undertake too much, then somehow get it done. Friendly, but often too absorbed in what they are doing to be sociable. Little concerned with possessions or physical surroundings.

I N T P

Quiet, reserved, brilliant in exams, especially in theoretical or scientific subjects. Logical to the point of hair-splitting. Usually interested mainly in ideas, with little liking for parties or small talk. Tend to have sharply defined interests. Need to choose careers where some strong interest can be used and useful.

INTROVERTS

E N F P

Warmly enthusiastic, high-spirited, ingenious, imaginative. Able to do almost anything that interests them. Quick with a solution for any difficulty and ready to help anyone with a problem. Often rely on their ability to improvise instead of preparing in advance. Can usually find compelling reasons for whatever they want.

E N T P

Quick, ingenious, good at many things. Stimulating company, alert and outspoken. May argue for fun on either side of a question. Resourceful in solving new and challenging problems, but may neglect routine assignments. Apt to turn to one new interest after another. Skillful in finding logical reasons for what they want.

E N F J

Responsive and responsible. Generally feel real concern for what others think or want, and try to handle things with due regard for other people's feelings. Can present a proposal or lead a group discussion with ease and tact. Sociable, popular, active in school affairs, but put time enough on their studies to do good work.

E N T J

Hearty, frank, able in studies, leaders in activities. Usually good in anything that requires reasoning and intelligent talk, such as public speaking. Are usually well-informed and enjoy adding to their fund of knowledge. May sometimes be more positive and confident than their experience in an area warrants.

EXTROVERTS

Briggs thumbnail sketches of each type are reprinted on pages 38–39.[1] Keep in mind that everyone will exhibit a particular trait at one time or another, but one type will fit you better than any of the others. You may want to refer to *Self Esteem—Gift from God* for more detailed help.

In my experience, Introverts and Sensing people usually know who and what they are. Extraverts and Intuitives are often unsure.

1. Reproduced by special permission of the publisher, Consulting Psychologists Press, Inc., Palo Alto, CA 94306, from *Myers Briggs Type Indicator* by Isabel Briggs Myers, © 1976. Further reproduction is prohibited without the publisher's consent.

2

God's Garden—Seedbed for Communication

Each one should test his own actions. Then he can take pride in himself, without comparing himself to somebody else, for each one should carry his own load. Galatians 6:4–5

Sometimes we are so aware of what we are not that we fail to appreciate what we are. Parents often approve of their offspring only when they are replicas of themselves, a very unfair and shortsighted view. Do you really want two of you? As hard as some of us might try, we just can't (or don't want to be) a carbon copy. This futile attempt can turn a home into the primary basis for low self-esteem.

A healthy self-image begins with accepting our personality and instinctive preferences—temperament—without complaint. Gladly! Enthusiastically! (I'm taking for granted that you readers have already come to terms with the "take what you get" features of physical appearance.) But, until we mature enough to understand that each person is unique in every way and possibly quite different from parents, siblings, spouse, and even friends, years of feeling inferior and weird are likely to mar our self-worth.

Unique as Flowers

Did you ever wonder why—as creative as God is—many people assume he merely created two kinds of people—male and female? How boring! And how untrue!

For hundreds of years society has stereotyped men as rough, rugged, and right and women as weak, weepy, and wrong. Only recently has our culture dared to accept behavior reflecting some men as innately softhearted and some women as tough-minded. Both male and female can share like temperaments, with excellent results if understood.

Consider the varieties of flowers that God has meticulously fashioned. The daffodil alone has more than forty varieties. Talk about individuality! Do you really think when it comes to humans that God would have limited his creativity to just two types?

Imagine flowers as having personalities that fill a garden with endless variety. Might we not hear that:

Geraniums desire to be delicate, like orchids?

Marigolds yearn to smell as sweet as gardenias?

Violets aspire to be hardy, like zinnias?

Petunias crave as bounteous a production as chrysanthemums?

Roses complain about their thorns?

Sunflowers dislike being up there all alone?

Human temperaments differ as much as flowers, although naturally the differences are extremely more complex. Subtle variations within like temperaments are also very distinguishable. No two people are exactly alike, even though they share the same temperament preferences in the four major areas discussed in the previous chapter.

A good illustration of this is found in my own family.

My sister, brothers and I share exactly the same preferences in temperament. We are very close in age and relationships and are drawn to the same interests. Yet we show distinct differences in the way we choose to use our preferences. Each person is unique.

As I have done in other books, I will use a well-known activity as an aid in making clear application of the truths we will discover. Since flowers, like music, speak a universal language, we will pretend that we are part of a huge flower garden—God's. Each temperament will be assigned a flower name that I think has a degree of resemblance—just an extra little handle for emphasis.

We will try to envision what growing in a flower garden with sixteen different varieties might be like. Each type needs sunshine, water, and nourishment—though in different amounts. They will all battle bugs, weeds, and normal garden woes. Some flowers may pair off, only to discover that their needs are different and that they require extra attention for blending. The real beauty of a flower garden is in the eye of the beholder, so some learned appreciation is in the offing.

We should have lots of fun observing these colorful, sensitive, but complex flowers. (Please don't press the analogy too far. I'm not a flower expert or much of a gardener, either.) Enjoy your flower type, realizing that no variety is either inferior or superior. If you are unhappy with the flower that describes your personality, feel free to substitute your favorite if it has similar characteristics. The last descriptive word or phrase after each flower is a general characteristic of that type, borrowed from *Self-Esteem—Gift from God.*

ISFJ— **Tulip.** Brilliantly colored, steady, organized: *Servers*

ISFP— **Rose.** Delicate and colorful, versatile, rambling, independent: *Sympathizers*

ISTJ— **Aster.** Tall and strong, bright and distinct: *Conscientious Workers*

ISTP— **Gladiolus.** Strong, colorful, independent important background for other flowers: *Unstoppable Operators*

ESFJ— **Zinnia.** Hardy, colorful, strong, popular, versatile: *Hostesses and Hosts*

ESFP— **Daisy** (means Day's Eye). Popular, brilliant, hardy, cheerful: *Performers*

ESTJ— **Geranium.** Sturdy, red, white, or pink, adaptable, hardy, dependable, well respected: *Organizers*

ESTP— **Hollyhock.** Tall, hardy, colorful, popular, needs sunlight, independent, adaptable: *Rescuers*

INFJ— **Camellias.** Delicate, has beautiful red, white, pink, or spotted rose-like blossoms and shiny dark green leaves, prefers shady spot: *Empathizers*

INFP— **Portulaca.** Colorful, delicate, complex, private, jubilant, many uses: *Idealists*

INTJ— **Iris.** Stately, unusual, brilliant, sturdy, roots have many uses: *Expert Strategists*

INTP— **Delphinium.** Delicate blossoms, usually blue, with a spur sticking up behind them on tall stems, independent: *Think-Tank Experts*

ENFJ— **Poppy.** Delicate beauty, hardy, yellow, rose-pink, scarlet, and other colors, versatile, popular: *Encouragers*

ENFP—**Chrysanthemum.** Hardy, bright and colorful, versatile, popular, good mixer: *Catalysts*

ENTJ— **Sunflower.** Overseer, strong, bright, positive, many uses: *Head Chief*

ENTP—**Hibiscus.** Large, fragrant, showy, seven-to-eight-foot stem, many uses: *Powerful People-Movers*

The Symptoms of Low Self-Esteem

Until we like how God made us, or at least understand and accept our unique gifting and that of the people with whom we live and work, we are not likely to share our ideas and encouragement with others or hear and appreciate their contributions.

Healthy self-esteem begins with getting acquainted with God's unique gifting without feeling apologetic about what we are. The cross-bearing evangelist Arthur Blessett said something like this: "When criticism and praise hit you the same, you're about right." I think this is a good measure for self-esteem.

Low self-esteem seems to be a worldwide malady of major proportions, surpassing alcoholism, drug abuse, lack of education, or money problems. Experiences in family counseling convinced me years ago that low self-esteem was at the root of many marriage failures, family grievances, church squabbles, and even poor mental and physical health. The rising number of suicides among teens can be traced in many cases to a flawed self-image.

James Dobson, nationally known clinical psychologist, family counselor, lecturer, and author, and Josh McDowell, a popular educator, speaker, and author (especially among the college crowd) have both stated the same conclusion.

Actually, the critical problem we all grapple with is lack of open and productive communication. If anyone ever gave you the silent treatment, you know what I mean. Inadequate or negative communication breeds isolation, misunderstandings, and feelings of rejection. It contributes little to friendships or problem solving. In fact, open communication is what strings people together and makes living worthwhile.

Good communication is not just casual conversation, but honest sharing and listening. Some risk may be involved in this. Satisfactory communication takes time, effort, mutual respect, courage, and healthy self-esteem. Edifying communication is a skill to be mastered.

The complaints I hear most often from unhappy counselees revolve around the absence of good communication:

"He comes home and reads the paper or watches the tube. He's not interested in what I have to say."

"She talks to her girlfriends on the phone, but sits in the living room hooked up to earphones when I'm around."

"The only time we ever talk is when we fight over money, sex, or relatives."

"My teenage daughter either disappears into her room or leaves for extracurricular activities or fun with her friends." (Teenagers say, "I just can't talk to my parents.")

"I don't understand my boss."

"My sister and I are on different wavelengths."

"The team just can't get along."

"No one understands me."

"Someone's feelings are always getting hurt at work."

A significant part of Feeling decision-makers' self-esteem hinges on hearing positive feedback about what they are, do, and say from bosses, spouses, parents, co-workers, or friends. These people tend to measure their worth by the amount of information others share with them.

Low self-esteem and lack of communication are inter-related. Recent articles blame many divorces directly on disenchanted spouses who want not more sex or security but communication. Lack of communication is often traced to our preoccupation with such fast-paced, single pursuits as running, aerobics, and working out, and to the disappearance of mealtimes—the natural setting for conversation.

A Case Study

Twila, a ten-year-old girl who was upsetting the family with chronic stomach pains and headaches, temper tantrums, and resistance to going to school, was merely suffering from a lack of positive communication and proper appreciation of her qualities.

As an Introverted-Intuitive-Feeling-Spontaneous child (INFP), Twila needed tender attention, constant approval, and encouragement. But the preferences of Twila's family were opposite from hers. Though also Introverted, they were Sensing, Thinking, and Structured (ISTJ) and regarded tantrums and immature behavior as manipulative, a little weird, inferior, and certainly unacceptable. They believed it was up to Twila to "grow up and fall in line." Envision a delicate *Portulaca* trying to blend with strong and tall *Asters!*

When they finally understood that Twila's hostility was a legitimate cry for praise, conversation, and tender-loving-care—all unnatural behavior for their own type—her family began to administer emotional first aid by taking new interest in her abilities and acknowledging the child's feelings and fears.

As Twila's angry outbursts gradually subsided, emotions stabilized in the household. With improved self-esteem, she was able to deal with her frustrations. Twila is now enthusiastically concentrating on those academic activities at school that can feed a healthy self-image in precocious little girls. Sensitive family communication was the key to removing her feelings of inferiority and setting her free as a person in her own right.

Baring One's Heart and Mind

Until a person understands and appreciates how and why others think, feel, and act, conversation will most likely be inappropriate or misinterpreted. And unless the person who desires to improve relationships is secure enough to risk being misunderstood or rejected, successful communication may remain a dream.

Communication Styles: Thinkers vs. Feelers

Thinkers (50 percent of the total population) prefer brief, logical verbal exchanges that are primarily situation-based rather than concerned with people and their feelings. They dislike wading through volumes of nonessential information that could be omitted or at least trimmed in the interest of relevancy.

Beating-around-the-bush decisions annoy decisive Thinkers, many of whom are apt to regard "good communication" as the absence of discussion and argument. Thinkers trust their decisions and expect others to do the same. They cannot agree to anything for which they do not see good reasons. "Don't ask questions, just do what I say" is most Thinkers' motto, but it is hardly very conducive to comfortable conversation. However, Thinkers need to admit that even "logical" decisions can often be improved.

Feeling decision-makers, who may be strangely attracted to Thinkers, often lack the courage and self-esteem to challenge cold logic. "I'm afraid to disagree," many Feelers have shared. Ironically, that people are afraid of them never ceases to amaze Thinkers, who actually regard themselves as fairly soft when necessary. Thinkers say they do not like to argue, but they just can't stand to be wrong. Don't be afraid of them! Take my word for it: they need and want your warmth, friendliness, and persistence.

Feelers, who are not eager to buck decisive Thinkers but want harmonious communication, first need to have their points and facts well in mind or on paper, then gather their courage and practice brevity as they converse with their opposites. In my experience, I have discovered that it takes at least two Feeling individuals to sway a Thinker's logic.

On the other hand, Thinkers do well to meet Feelers halfway by learning to tolerate a dose of nonessentials and endeavor to soften their bluntness. "If I would just hear him say 'I love you' once in a while, I would feel so much better," a Feeling wife might say, though her Thinking husband would probably respond, "I don't have to repeat something that hasn't changed."

Normally, Thinkers are rather confident and need only occasional verbal approval of who they are or what they have already decided or accomplished. If they are to open the communication channels, they need to learn to verbally affirm their counterparts regularly until it becomes a habit.

"The house is a mess. I'm not used to that," Bill griped to his wife. "What did you do all day, for heaven's sake?" Bill sees no tangible sign of housekeeping excellence and smells no food cooking—all familiar memories from his childhood.

Jan feels intimidated by his loaded question, so she becomes obstinate and private about her activities. "I'm not against housework," Jan defended. "I've been working all day helping Mrs. Dillon. She needed a ride home from the hospital and her house needed attention. So *that's* what I've been doing! I feel helping her is more important than doing something for ourselves," she added sarcastically.

Bill needs to applaud Jan, a Feeling person who would put in thirty-six straight hours of caring for someone in need without a complaint. But she also needs his approval for doing that.

Thinkers could quell much intimidation and also improve their image and popularity by affirming "I love you" more often, occasionally admitting when they are wrong, and saying "I'm sorry" or "I think you are a super person" when appropriate. Any person who desires the dividends of trust and respect must invest in the virtues of consideration and tenderness.

Put Thinking and Introversion together and you have the quietest people in the world! Introvert-Thinkers are not actually anti-dialogue, but find talking quite draining, even painful. Many times, such people come across as stern, unfriendly, and no-nonsense. Even though sharing personal feelings is unnatural for them, they will respond readily when they discover someone with whom they can entrust their confidences.

Introvert-Thinkers need to understand how their silence intimidates the Feeling segment—including those who are confident Extraverts—and should also consider how important it is to their friends, co-workers, and especially their spouses and children, to hear their voices, share ideas, feelings, and foolishness, and do a little laughing.

Extravert-Thinkers can more easily tolerate people and conversation, but they, too, prefer brief, logical discussions. Because they rely on "ear editing" somewhat, they periodically put their foot in their mouth.

Thinkers need to endeavor to listen to more chatter than they would normally choose and share tidbits of this-and-that so as to comply somewhat with Feeling people's expectations and their gauge of personal worth.

The other 50 percent of the world—Feeling decision-makers of both genders—require small talk but also hunger for in-depth communication. Although it is not their favorite kind of conversation, Feelers are quite capable of consulting logic when appropriate.

Feeling people can rightly be titled "information bearers," for as soon as they receive interesting data they have a compulsion to pass it along. Because warmhearted people find it easy to share news, even when the subject has not come up naturally, many need to develop discipline in discretionary sharing.

Feelers are constantly wondering if they are meeting with the approval of others and would like to be told, especially when they do, since they have a tendency to measure their worth by what their counterparts share with them. They appreciate verbal praise for who they are, for products made and services rendered and say to others what they expect to hear or have done in return.

Since few Thinkers understand the complexity of Feelers' expectations—spoken and unspoken—the latter suffer tremendously and needlessly from hurt feelings, anger, resentments, and low self-esteem. (The bulk of this book addresses these problems.) On the other hand, harmony lovers need to keep in mind that insisting on peace at any price may also be shortcutting someone else's growth in maturity and responsibility.

When the softhearted are also Introverts, they prefer limited conversation and fewer people. Communication is not easy for them, yet they need it so much! Usually they prefer talking with one person at a time. Many find it easier to put their feelings and opinions on paper. They are usually very patient listeners who attract Extraverts who want to talk.

Quiet and sensitive men, women, boys, and girls are unlikely to reveal their emotional needs without some encouragement. Thus, without others' knowledge, their self-esteem often drastically drags bottom, making them easy targets for depression. That might explain why the majority of counseling is done with this group.

Extraverted Feelers are the talkers of this world. In fact, they have a tendency to drown everyone in words. Unfortunately, some of these people have difficulty listening because they are so busy planning what they want to say next.

The Extravert-Sensing-Feelers are the truly loquacious ones. They want conversation and people nearly all the time and usually admit they can talk the ears off almost anyone. Mere ability to talk, however, does not mean that one appreciates or utilizes the skills of communication. (A good habit in serious dialogue is to repeat what the speaker just said: "I hear you saying. . . ." This not only teaches us to listen carefully but guarantees that listeners have sifted accurately through extensive verbiage.)

Because Feeling people are sensitive to criticism and are easily put on the defensive, many are often verbally at each other's throats when decisions are involved. Skilled dialogue modifies many such clashes. Since the Feeling population desires harmony and peaceful communication and is willing to patiently soothe, encourage, and counsel through written and spoken word, Thinkers should be willing to do their part in appreciating them and emulating their sensitivity.

Communication Styles: Intuitives vs. Sensers

A person's favorite way of gathering information also influences the kind of conversation he or she most appreciates. The Sensing crowd prefers chronological data—a linear description of facts, and events as they actually occurred. Their factual account of stories and events will nearly always be accurate and make sense, and they can repeat these stories exactly. Their Intuitive friends prefer to relate facts or discuss ideas helically—in a spiral or circular fashion that hits the high points first and saves supporting facts until last.

Repeating something verbatim is not only difficult for Intuitives, but also very boring. The facts, names, and fall of events may alter when repeated, not because these people are deceitful, but because Intuitives prefer to emphasize principles or present the big picture rather than touch upon details.

Though Intuitives are often suspected of tampering with the truth, they usually do so unintentionally, because they honestly don't remember "how much" or "when." Of course, anybody, no matter what type, is capable of deliberately misstating facts or stretching the truth. (We will not deal with that issue in this volume.)

When you know what type of person you are addressing, transferring information according to the method the other prefers will aid communication. Hopefully, he or she will do the same for you!

Couples who pair an Intuitive with a Senser may experience poor communication because they are in different arenas. Even if they are both also Extraverts, they need help in learning how to relate to and receive information from their partner. For example, I attempt to get all my facts straight before I discuss a new idea or purchase with Jim, who is Sensing in temperament. I usually list the items on paper. It's easier for me to talk in his style than to expect him to adjust to my circular way of conversation.

Probably the best communicators are Extraverts who also prefer to operate on Intuitive and Feeling levels (ENF). However, although they regard people as being of highest importance and priority, they may take communication for granted, believing that they are understood and that their explanations and ideas are accepted. Extravert-Intuitives are usually able to talk their own and others' problems through with ease.

Communication Styles: Structured vs. Spontaneous People

Conversation, and thus communication, is also affected by a person's choice of lifestyle. Structured people like to know things ahead of time so that they have time to think over facts and details and "get ready." Spontaneous people become burdened with too much beforehand information and have a tendency to forget details. This is probably because they are always sitting on "go" and want nothing to threaten their freedom of action.

My research shows that Spontaneous people seem to enjoy the process of conversation, whereas Structured people just want to get it finished and move on to the next item on their agenda. Many Structured counselees complain that the Spontaneous people in their lives choose to discuss a problem "right now" rather than scheduling a talk for later, when there would be sufficient or quality time.

Watering the Seedbed

The miraculous improvement in communication after people understand how God has designed differences in temperament leaves no doubt that we are on the right track in building self-esteem. Until we respect ourselves, we will not really respect anyone else, either. True, the response we get from others does affect our self-esteem, but if the foundation of our self-image is based on recognizing God's unique gifting, we are better prepared to adjust to others' lack of appreciation for us as individuals.

Healthy self-esteem is God's plan for everyone. When Jesus said, "Love others as you love yourself," he assumed that our acceptance and appreciation of ourselves would be projected toward others in positive actions and words— through the water of communication.

Next to air, water is the most important necessity for existence, yet is so often taken for granted that we seldom realize how essential or precious it is until the well runs dry. Bitter battles have been fought for the possession of some muddy waterhole or tiny stream. So, too, do emotionally thirsty people search for water—life-refreshing communication—for their dry, neglected, and crushed spirits.

In order to have a beautiful garden, one doesn't just aimlessly sow seeds or dump bulbs on the ground and then sit back and watch something gorgeous happen. A healthy array of flowers is the result of soil preparation, pruning, fertilizing, spraying, weeding, tilling and, certainly, skillful watering. The same principles apply as we blend the temperamentally unique specimens in God's garden of humanity.

Applying understanding and appreciation is like mixing light and air with water to assure a garden's growth. The goal of this book is to increase the understanding and appreciation that encourage effective communication, with the overall aim of improving the quality of relationships at all levels. These ideas have been tested and tried by hundreds of people. They work!

3

Expectations—
Bugs in Our Garden

A man's spirit sustains him in sickness, but a crushed spirit who can bear? The heart of the discerning acquires knowledge; the ears of the wise seek it out. Proverbs 18:14–15

This book is written for those who want to achieve, who desire to do their best and realize their potential, but also for those who wish to encourage others to make the most of the priceless gift of life, their abilities and personality.

The information I have gathered from every type of person, from various economic and educational backgrounds and assorted age groups, indicates that expectations are somewhat like bugs in a garden. There are lots of them. Everywhere, and in various shapes and colors. Some bugs are beneficial and some are destructive; some are big and some so small they can barely be seen.

Like bugs, expectations—whether subtle, unspoken, imagined, or expressed—wield almost unbelievable influence on communication and life itself. Identifying the various categories is a necessary first step toward building and maintaining healthy self-esteem in ourselves and others.

If we did a word-association test on expectations, the responses would range from positive to strongly negative. Certain expectations are healthy and good. For example, encouraging children to love to learn and to respect hard work is the privileged duty of parents and teachers. Urging young people to aim high and realize their potential so as to be independent and successful is a built-in assignment that has its own rewards for adults. All this involves developing the right kind of expectations.

Granted, some people set no goals or put any expectations on themselves or their children, perhaps because no one held out any reachable expectations for them. Others seem to require no outside encouragement to strive for excellence. There are also those who are faithfully and positively challenged but still choose mere survival. When a person's self-esteem is low or unhealthy, he or she usually does not plan for the future or set challenging personal goals.

Some expectations may come across as threatening and vindictive and thereby produce guilt, inadequacy, anger, and resentment, which can kill the spirits of anyone in their grip. Expecting children to be Number One may

frighten them into underachievement. A fine line of balance must be drawn between aspirations and "reality," which includes one's abilities and temperament.

David's dad, a doctor, insisted his son always wear coat and tie to school because someday he would be a doctor or perhaps a lawyer, like his uncle. Although dressing up was not in style at David's school, he obeyed Dad's rules. However, David eventually chose not to go to college and now runs a successful little business where he wears tennis shoes and a T-shirt.

Understanding variety in temperament provides clues toward the kind of expectations and challenges others are likely to appreciate and respond to. For instance, most Intuitives would find it very frustrating to be expected to excel in a Sensing, hands-on occupation. Pete described his experiences:

> I tried my dad's business, but failed. He's the VP of a national lending institution and wanted me to step into a financially secure career like my brother did. But I just couldn't get into figures and offices. I wanted to please him and didn't want to seem ungrateful, but it just didn't work. We got on each other's nerves. I just wasn't happy. I do enjoy designing home interiors, though. I don't make as much, but I look forward to going to work. Dad still doesn't understand. He says, "Someday you'll come around."

Children who reject involvement in a family business or parent's profession often create a bitter pill for their elders to swallow, but many family feuds are avoided when parents recognize that their offspring may have different expectations from their own.

Many Sensing people directed and shoved toward Intuitive careers such as counseling or the ministry experience the same level of frustration, as did Rick, who explained:

All my brothers are ministers. My parents have told me a million times that at birth they dedicated me for full-time religious work. But I am not that comfortable around people and really enjoy being a CPA. Even though I am the treasurer for our church, that doesn't satisfy them.

Some parents are extremely disappointed and fearful when their children resist going to college or fail while there. Of course, college isn't for everyone, but a college education in most cases is a wise investment of time and money for most. The discipline of study and exposure to learning prepare students for an unknown future.

Just as some people are better off in non-college pursuits, others are more fulfilled by remaining single and/or childless. Heavy family expectations in these areas produce disappointment, disagreement, and eventually deep-seated resentment on both sides.

Self-Imposed Expectations

Nearly everyone says at one time or another, "I *should* do [or be] this or that." Self-imposed expectations are helpful when they involve such goals as planning a career, pursuing an education, learning a job, getting up for work, studying for a test, finishing a project, taking care of children or possessions. Unfortunately, a great many people spend their lives correcting mistakes or enslaved to appetites that require tremendous support. Sometimes a person is kept from doing what he or she really enjoys doing until rather late in life.

If you have chosen to be a parent, student, employee, or provider and later discover you don't *want* to do the things you have obligated yourself to do, you must work on changing your "wanter." Motivating ourselves to accomplish what falls within our responsibility is synonymous with maturity. The energizing stress that comes from doing what appeals to us or is in line with reachable goals is a positive innovator that even the most Structured and self-confident person relies on.

Basically, human beings are lazy. It surprises many of us to discover that even highly Structured people sometimes have to scold and cajole themselves into doing what they know is theirs to do. We all struggle with having to change our "wanters." Being consistently disciplined is a tough assignment for everyone.

Sensing people have a tendency to procrastinate dealing with emotional responsibilities, while Intuitives may have to muster up more motivation when the obligation involves physical routine. The Spontaneous crowd, usually very responsive to unexpected and exciting challenges, is obliged to struggle more than anyone in this area. You see, we're all basically in the same pickle, regardless of our temperament.

Scott Peck, in *The Road Less Travelled,* goes so far as to identify original sin as laziness. The opposite of laziness is not perfection, Peck says, but love. His perspective is refreshing and right on target.

The kind of self-imposed expectations we most want to analyze here are those that are unrealistic, or in opposition to our particular type of temperament, and thus produce harmful stress, which destroys self-confidence and inhibits communication. The bad kind of bugs in our garden!

Many of us are guilty of deciding what we want to be or do without regard for our particular situation or temperament. We are then disappointed if we don't or can't measure up to our mental goal or standard in such ways as these:

"I should keep the house as perfect as when I didn't have an outside job."

"I must maintain straight A's at night school, even
though I work full time."

"I've gotta make a certain number of sales this week."

"I must not be like my irresponsible father in any way."

"Since my sister blew it, I'm determined to make my
folks proud of me."

"I need to maintain the standard of living my parents
had."

"The children deserve my unlimited time."

"Everyone must like me."

"I should make all my presents, like my sister does."

"I'm going to reach the top financially."

"My opinions and ideas must be highly respected by all
my friends."

Many women employed outside the home put unrealistic expectations on themselves to be super moms and
wives. It is humanly improbable, even in a two-parent
family, to work forty hours a week away from home, prepare balanced meals, assist children with homework, fulfill chauffeuring duties, and still have some private time
for self, spouse, and friends.

Our society teems with single parents who are inclined
to compensate totally for the absence of the other parent
and thus subject themselves to guilt-producing unreasonable expectations. These people, predominantly women,
eventually suffer low self-esteem and experience burnout.

Many men unconsciously struggle to disprove what Dad
always said—"You'll never amount to anything"—by
working fifty-sixty hours a week. Others are pressured by
the educational, prestigious, or financial achievements of
their siblings or parents. It is a given that most children
vie for parental blessing, often unsuccessfully. Surprisingly, many adults struggle all their lives to get the ap-

proval of parents. All they really want to hear is "I'm proud of you and love you." Some of these unexamined expectations must be settled posthumously with counseling. (*The Power to Bless* by Myron C. Madden offers excellent counsel on this special problem.)

Introverts tend to lay on themselves the goal of *never* failing. Thinkers often contend relentlessly for success, trust, and respect by their peers and superiors. Many Feelers aim to satisfy and please everyone, striving for faultless living so they will be liked by one and all.

"Do you tolerate anyone, Sandy?" I asked a counselee.

"Yes," she said sheepishly.

"Do you suppose, then, that anyone has to tolerate you?"

"Oh, I hope not," Sandy shivered. "I want everyone to like me."

"We don't like *ourselves* all the time. How can we expect others to like us all the time?" I questioned.

"I don't know," Sandy hesitated. "I guess I just assumed that good people are liked by all."

If you expect yourself never to say a disagreeable word or dislike anyone, you'll never like or approve of yourself totally.

"When we don't measure up to our own expectations," an Intuitive group member shared, "we are likely to get discouraged with who we are and want to throw in the towel."

A pastor's wife recently shared that learning that it was permissible to tolerate others and to expect others to tolerate her really released her from guilt at her church. "It's okay, now, that others don't particularly like me," she said with confidence. "As a result, I like myself a whole lot more," she added with a grin.

Intuitives have to be especially careful to separate expectations from idealistic aspirations. We all need goals of some kind, but setting unreal expectations for ourselves is most often counterproductive.

Structured people—whether Sensing or Intuitive—have

been known to make lists a mile long for Saturday, their
only day off. When they don't complete it for whatever
good (or bad) reason, they condemn themselves. They seldom leave time for play and become angry with themselves for not completing their scheduled tasks.

Spontaneous people seem better able to resist the daily
pressure of self-imposed expectations because of their
characteristic resistance to schedules and plans. But they
will still suffer overall self-condemnation if their responsibilities or achievements fall below what they expected
of themselves.

Analyze your self-imposed expectations to make sure
you are being realistic. Many of the things we expect ourselves to do, say, or become are unreasonable—unless we
are in training for Superman (or Superwoman) of the Year.
Self-drawn expectations are rarely challenged by others,
so we need to learn to ask ourselves:

Is this something I really want?

What is my motivation for wanting this?

Why do I expect myself to achieve these goals?

Is that a reasonable expectation for myself?

Does the outcome warrant the energy expended?

Does the expectation violate my temperament preferences?

Am I physically and mentally able to fulfill this expectation?

Is my personal expectation hurting others?

Does it really add depth and meaning to my life?

Imagined Expectations

Many of our expectations are superfluous since they
reflect only our *imagined* concept of aspirations others

have set before us. (Feelers seem to have more problems with imagined expectations because they are so eager to please others and receive approval.)

Some of our imagined expectations parallel the list of the self-imposed ones already described. We may assume someone else expects us to do something, when this is not so. For example, I have always taken personal pride in unlocking the door when I heard Jim drive up, knowing that he usually had his hands full, and greeting him with a cheery hello and a kiss. (I like the kiss and think he does, too!) I've done this for years because I wanted to and also because I thought he expected me to. However, when involved in a counseling session, I usually found it awkward and a bit rude to interrupt serious dialogue by jumping up to unlock the door. On occasion I would disregard the noise of Jim's key in the lock and try to ignore my sense of guilt for not unlocking the door for him. I feared he would think my clients were more important than he was, and I didn't want him to resent my counseling.

One day, I decided to test my own suggestions about handling mixed emotions by checking out the validity of my assumed expectations, so I asked, "Jim, do you expect me to unlock the door?"

"No, I don't," he said. "In fact, it bothers me when you do because I already have my keys out."

My guilt was lessening, but my feelings were a little hurt at his answer, and I challenged, "But I thought you expected me to greet you whenever you came home."

"That's *your* idea," he said. "Actually, I feel a bit crowded when you meet me. I'm usually deep in thought and prefer a little space."

That completely released me. Jim still seeks me out and greets me with a kiss, which pleases me, but I don't feel pressured anymore. However, when I'm the one coming in at night, Jim knows that I like to be greeted and assisted with packages at the door. I had just assumed that he did, too. But Thinkers are not as sensitive as Feelers about being greeted and assisted! (I *have* discovered that some Thinking Intuitives do like their spouses to greet them at the door. Intuitives like to feel important.)

Let's analyze another example. . . .

Many pastors' wives imagine that parishioners expect them to attend every meeting, teach classes, serve in the nursery, keep a perfect home, have flawless kids, an ideal marriage, always wear a smile, and present a positive attitude about everything.

One informal survey revealed that these were not normal expectations imposed by all parishioners, although some did hold higher standards for ministers' families. So what if they do? Is that fair? No one can satisfy an entire congregation. But just assuming that these high expectations are held has injured many pastors' families. In other words, they have created much of their own stress. As a side note, the survey astoundingly revealed that a great number of *pastors* were guilty of expecting these things from their wives, but this is a subject for another book.

Pastors' wives are not alone in being stressed by imagined expectations, as this next example proves. Harry, a conscientious teacher, shared:

> My co-teachers have asked me every year, "What job have you found for the summer? I realize, after all these years, that rather than taking the summers to read, relax, study, and prepare curriculum for the next year, I've given in to peer pressure and found a job because I supposed, since my co-workers expected it, that it was the right thing to do. I feel certain that I've unknowingly done my personality a great deal of harm over the years by not following my personal preferences. From now on, I intend to adjust my summer schedule to meet *my* personal goals.

Harry's teacher friends have no idea what pressure they unconsciously exerted on their co-worker. "It's my problem," Harry admitted. "I chose to be controlled by what I imagined were others' expectations. Yet I resented and blamed them for those unfulfilling summers. It feels good to finally be in charge of making my own vacation decisions."

The truth is, trying to live up to expectations that we *imagine* others have put on us is pressure that could eventually put us in the mental ward. It is obvious that we need to distinguish between imagined and real expectations. Just a little bit of checking with the person or group we imagine has placed an expectation before us will clear the air and relieve tension as well as encourage creative communication. Asking ourselves those "what" and "why" questions can purify our motives and release us from any self-made boxes of guilt.

Unspoken Expectations We Put on Others

Many people create their own problems by setting up unreasonable expectations for others to fulfill and then keeping those expectations a mystery—like Lois Nelson. . . .

The Nelsons are in business together. Lois's expectations of Larry have been unreasonable in many respects. She likes to be with him and appreciates his business skills, but she's hard to please. Lois expects him to say just the right thing (by *her* standards). She prefers that Larry stay in the inner office, to keep him away from customers to whom he might say something she doesn't approve of. Lois needs to keep in mind that because Larry is an Extravert, he will likely say things she (an Introvert) regards as unnecessary.

This wife expects her husband to do the "proper" thing by helping her only when she wants help (which would require that he read her mind, since she doesn't talk very easily). Lois needs to *tell* Larry what she expects of him. Then he can tell her whether or not he can deliver.

Lois also thinks that Larry only pretends not to know what is going on around him. She complains that he doesn't pick up what she regards as strong hints about things that need doing, but she needs to remember that because Larry is an Intuitive, he will not be as observant as she is about the physical world. Larry gets lost in the idea world from time to time, which is quite normal for an Intuitive.

Here's another example of how unspoken expectations can cause problems. . . .

"I expect John to come right home after work," Lila said. "But I can call him at three to make sure he's coming home on time and he'll say yes, then won't show up until eight."

"How long has he been telling you that he'll be home right after work?" I asked.

"For years." (Lila had already told me that if she cooks and John doesn't show, she resents his being late. "I like to serve him a hot dinner," she had explained.)

"How often does he show up late?"

"About every Friday," she shrugged.

"What would you do if you knew he wouldn't be coming home for dinner?" was my next question.

"I'd go ahead and eat a sandwich alone and use my time on something else. I'd go see our daughter or go out with a friend, lots of things."

Here was my suggestion: "Why not claim Friday as your night off, then, and plan not to cook unless John specifically says he will be there. If he comes home unexpectedly and dinner is not prepared, let him take you out to eat. That is, if you don't have other plans."

John, a Spontaneous Intuitive, gets bored when events are too routine, so he creates crises, though Lila tries to prevent them. He likes to stir the pot when life bubbles smoothly along. If Lila seems too easygoing, he stays out late to stir things up. Yet, to change herself to satisfy his hunger for excitement violates Lila's Structured and Sensing preferences for predictability.

If John intimidates Lila, he will lose respect for her. There is no need for her to boss him around, but she must stand up for herself. She is not going to pity herself—that's childish. John will respect Lila when she respects herself and realizes that she does not have to apologize for who or how she is. John's inconsideration is partly because his wife has allowed herself to be intimidated, rather than making plain what she expects of him.

Dr. Kevin Leman, discussing this in *The Birth Order Book,* says there is no way you can directly change anybody else's behavior. You can only change your own behavior, and when you do make a genuine effort to do that, the strangest things can happen: other people in your life will make the behavioral changes you have been hoping for all along.

Expectations that we put on others without informing them (or that others privately put on us) cause tremendous problems in communication. When we assume that certain things will be said or done and those expectations go unfulfilled, many of us, especially Feeling people, are likely to get upset and hurt and suffer rejection or resentment. Thinkers are more likely to just be bothered and disappointed. A question like "Where were you last night? We came to see you" lays guilt on the people who were away. These visitors actually expected their relatives to be home and are unjustifiably resentful because they were not.

Does your Sensing husband glare at you when you hand him the phone backwards, tangling the cord? Laugh it off as one of your little inefficiencies as an Intuitive rather than an inept failure. Rather than smolder in secret or lash out in verbal defense, enlist some humor: "I can't be beautiful and a perfect phone handler at the same time." Then promise you'll try to do better next time.

Elaine came from a home where no arguments were allowed, yet disagreements in her husband's home were as normal as hugs and kisses. This couple will need to discuss their differences openly and arrive at creative compromise.

"My husband expects me to take care of him when he's sick, just like his mother did," Phyllis complained. "He's such a baby. But I didn't know that when I married him. And he certainly doesn't respond that way to me when *I'm* sick."

Some people (especially those who make decisions by Feeling) seem to expect others to mistreat them. They even help them out by constantly condemning and faulting themselves. These people need to communicate their expectations so others can either reject the expectations or embrace the now-spoken desires. Criticism follows when expectations are unmet, or any time someone is put on the defensive. The following examples also take the smile out of relationships:

Expecting club officers to function like their predecessors

Expecting that employees will always turn in reports on time

Expecting children to keep their rooms straight

Expecting guests to check your schedule before they come

Expecting written acknowledgment for a gift

Expecting unlimited baby-sitting by grandparents

Once someone renders a service, benefitters are likely to assume that it is part of the regular program, as in these situations:

Making the coffee at work

Calling in the lunch order

Running forgotten items to school

Washing clothes

Waking family members for work or school

Picking up clutter

Preparing meals

Answering the phone(s)

Locking or unlocking the doors

Fueling and maintaining vehicles

Keeping up the yard

Running errands

Compile your own list of expectations that you assume others put on you, and then one for unspoken expectations that you put on other people. This could be a fun family-or-work exercise and is excellent for stimulating communication. It can relieve family tensions if creative compromises are considered and discussed by all concerned.

Thinkers generally figure that people do something because they like to do it or accept it as their duty. If no one complains, Thinkers assume that everything is okay and that the "workers" are happy. By way of contrast, Feeling people primarily say and do for others what they themselves want to hear and have done. When others don't reciprocate or even appreciate their services, they feel mistreated and unappreciated.

The Bible instructs us to "do to others what you would have them do to you [the Golden Rule]" (Matt. 7:12). Many Feelers might respond, "I do and do for others, and no one does for me." No one likes being taken for granted.

"Every time you need a pat on the back, give it to yourself and consider it from me," one Thinker said to his wife. "I'll tell you when I'm displeased with you," he promised. That sort of attitude is not enough for Feeling people, especially those who believe that they go beyond the call of duty in the many little things they feel obligated to do—even though they enjoy being needed.

Many women hold their breath before a special day,

hoping against hope that the day will be remembered by loved ones. Feeling hearts ache when they receive no birthday cake, Valentine card, or Mother's Day gift. It should come as no surprise that Feeling men and boys expect the same kind of attention, praise, appreciation, and thanks that "softhearted" females do.

It is hard enough to fulfill expressed expectations, but to hope that others will read our minds is unrealistic and even unfair.

Expressed Expectations

Expectations that are expressed in one way or another are the easiest kind to identify and deal with. They come in assorted styles and can both communicate desires and engender a variety of reactions.

Blunt Statements

"I wish you were more like your sister."

"Honey, the baby is crying."

"I expect you to call as soon as you arrive."

"These reports must go out tonight." (Or other statements including "ought to," "should," "need to.")

"I expected you to clean up your mess."

"I Thought"-Type Statements

"I thought you would wait for me."

"I assumed you'd get me up."

"I figured you were going to pay for it."

"I thought you would at least call me."

"I supposed that was your job, not mine."

Statements that Are Questions

"You're coming for Thanksgiving this year, aren't you?"

"Mom, you washed my jeans, didn't you?"

"Don't you ever look at the gas gauge?" (This is a type of sarcasm dealt with in *Encouragement—A Wife's Special Gift* [Baker Book House, 1979].

"We can count on you to be there, can't we?"

"You don't mind catching my phone, do you?"

"You don't mind handling those details, do you?"

All these statements reek with guilt trips, especially to people with a Feeling temperament. Thinkers are apt to respond with "You thought wrong" or "So what!" or something else that means they are rejecting the other person's expectation.

My research shows that Feeling people, who wince more from presumptuous expectations, are also more likely to place expectations—subtle and not so subtle—on others. A Thinking person will usually be forthright about what he or she expects. If you ask Thinkers, "What do you expect?" they will usually give you a straight answer.

Many expectations surface only during disagreements, which is why careful listening is so important. Capitalizing on these discoveries promotes communication and leads to creative compromise, thus strengthening the bonds of love and relationships at all levels.

The Expectation Trap

Differences in temperament underlie the bulk of interpersonal problems because we neither all require the same kind of appreciation and attention or see what needs to be done in the same way. As we have seen, each type of person also has a particular style of doing things. Knowledge about temperaments equips us to perceive others' expectations as well as understand our own.

The old adage "Doing what you don't like to do builds character" reflects much wisdom, but some people go too far in expecting themselves to accomplish *most* of the time that which exceeds their abilities, available time, physical and mental energies, or natural inclinations. This leads to self-dissatisfaction as well as resentment toward those who expect (or we imagine as expecting) certain performance. Eventually there is burnout, so we need to be realistic about what we can honestly deliver or achieve.

Expectations of all kinds have to be understood and confronted and sometimes rejected. Otherwise, guilt, anger, and resentment occur, and any of those emotions can be unhealthy.

People who feel guilty when they realize that they have not fulfilled their own or someone else's expectations must learn to recognize that a particular expectation may be unfair or inappropriate for them. Just because you feel guilty does not mean that you are.

4

Grappling with Guilt— Destructive Insects

Let us draw near to God with a sincere heart in full assurance of faith, having our hearts sprinkled to cleanse us from a guilty conscience. . . . Hebrews 10:22

We have seen that unfulfilled expectations leave a residue of hurt feelings, irritation, and inadequacy. All these are roadblocks to effective communication, but next we will examine ways to deal with the most telltale effect of "bad bugs" in our garden—guilt and its poisonous results.

When others let us know in one way or another that we have failed to live up to their expectations by not acting a certain way or doing a particular thing, or we have fallen short of our own expectations, we are likely to be nagged and even tortured with a sense of guilt. Especially tender targets for this poisonous emotion are those of a Feeling temperament.

Softhearted people tend to yield more readily to others' thoughtless and unfair expectations because they hunger for harmony, want to please everyone, and are instinctively empathetic with the feelings and ideas of others.

Thinking people have a certain resiliency to taking guilt trips. They certainly have to be sent there by someone else, because they rarely elect to go on their own. For example, if a Thinker neglects to arrive on time, he (or she) may be very apologetic and even feel badly about being late, since he is disappointed with himself, but guilty feelings would probably not be one of his problems.

"Yes, I suppose I feel guilt at times," one Thinking man said, "if it's inflicted on me. If it's something I can help, I may suffer a little bit of guilt over it."

"Would sermons about how long it has been since you brought your wife a flower make you feel guilty?" I asked.

"No, that would just be a reminder to be more sensitive in the future," he reasoned.

No question about it: Thinking people do experience some hint of guilt for not pleasing others, and they prefer harmony to discord. But "peace at any price" is not their motto, mainly because they do not need others' approval to function. Thinkers want appreciation but (unlike Feeling people) generally do not subconsciously bait others for positive feedback. They are usually satisfied with self-approval. Though Thinkers appreciate approval after they have made decisions, they can even live without that if necessary.

In no way do I want to give the impression that Thinkers are not caring, sensitive, helpful, or others-oriented. They are just more private about expressing or seeking affection, and their logic-based decisions protect them from assuming guilt or blame unless irrefutable facts prove otherwise.

Since Feeling people instinctively regulate what they do and say by what they think the person they want to please expects, they unconsciously set themselves up for abuse, paralleling the insidious attacks of harmful insects on the sensitive leaves and stems of plants.

Trying to speak and act according to another's whims puts the other person in control of your self-esteem. You are really saying, "I'll be your mental and physical slave if you'll give me approval." Feeling people actually writhe in guilt when others disapprove, criticize, or blame them. Their mental anguish is devastating, even when they are innocent. This is one of the main reasons many people seek counseling.

Guilt registers an especially heavy blow when adult children blame their parents for their social or emotional problems. Mothers, especially, often experience depression after such accusations. Unfortunately, homes that benefit one child often violate another. I've not met many people who boast of a perfect childhood. Was yours? By the time most people master parenthood, the children no longer live at home. Parental guilt is a poison that doesn't just dissolve. It must be dealt with and neutralized.

Misunderstood feelings and emotions can whirl people around in endless circles. Feeling people can learn to control their emotions and change their thinking by understanding the source and validity of their guilt trips.

The Guilt-Producing Process

Inadequacy and feelings of inferiority are two of the most destructive components of guilt. Ironically, a person may believe he or she is inferior simply because someone of a different temperamental makeup unintentionally implies it is so. For example, without meaning to, Extraverts cause feelings of inferiority to well up in Introverts when they expect them to speak up or be more assertive. "Teachers always mention how quiet our children are, as though we didn't know it," Judith said. "The children are beginning to think something is really wrong with them because they are not noisy like most of the others."

On the other hand, Introverts can induce feelings of inadequacy in Extraverts if they fault them for their inability to speak without making errors or refer to them as "blabbermouths." Feeling-Extraverts may appear to be thick-skinned but they easily bruise by name calling—a cruel type of rejection that is used in many homes, incidentally.

Sensing people arouse Intuitives' concept of inadequacy when they ridicule their ineptness with hands-on projects. "Why, he can't even find the hood of his car," a Senser may joke.

"My mother can't understand why I don't sew my children's clothes," Annie complained. "I want her to be proud of me, but I just can't get into sewing. I feel so guilty and inferior because my older sister makes all of her clothes." Many Intuitives already struggle to compete with Sensing people's productivity. No need to rub it in!

Intuitives can incite inferior feelings in Sensing people merely by bouncing so easily from one theory after another in a discussion, or speaking in fragments of sentences that hit only the high spots. "I stay away from that group," Tom said. "I'm just not on their wavelength. They lose me, and I'm afraid they're going to ask my opinion on some intellectual issue."

Many Sensing people feel generally inferior in the area of Intuitives' analytical ability, which resembles interrogation. Since Intuitives' natural talent for wiggling out of things often gives the false impression that they "know everything," they need to avoid intentional manipulations.

Structured people, without thinking, often imply that their Spontaneous opposites are lazy and disorganized by poking fun at them. "Haven't you finished laying your walk yet—or are you praying for snow?" they might tease.

Spontaneous people get their licks in, too, by such tactics as sermonizing a burned-out workaholic: "You should have gone fishing with me. I told you to take time to relax." Or they might try to get a Structured person off schedule: "Come with us. You're no fun at all and are in a deep dull rut. You'll be old before your time."

Regardless of temperament, many mothers—and some

dads—feel inadequate when they compare their children's achievements or growth with others. This guilt often develops into jealousy.

What guilt are *you* bearing? Make your list. This is the first step in tossing it away and erasing its destructive effects.

A Case Study in Guilt

Guilt catches us off guard at subtle times, as the following account by Tana illustrates:

> I received a call after my bedtime one Saturday evening from my friend Linda saying, "Tana, would you like to join my aerobics club? I need to know right now, and our next class is on Monday night. We meet for an hour and half. I can get you in for half price."
>
> I struggled to respond to the urgency of the call as I was waking up. My friend went on to say, "I know you will really enjoy this, and since I am next on the list to invite a friend, I get in for half price, too. But I must know *now* to call the teacher" and on and on. I paused a moment and then said, "Yes, I'll join."
>
> On Monday evening I reluctantly left our infant son with my husband, who just arrived home from a trip. I knew I would not enjoy this class for several reasons— the evening schedule, the length of the class, and the type of exercise. I prefer outdoor tennis.
>
> So, realizing this was not for me, I called Linda the next day to suggest that perhaps someone else would take my place and enjoy the opportunities more than I would. She became very upset with me and said, "If you drop out I'll look bad because one other girl I took dropped out, too."
>
> After saying how hurt she would be, that she would probably even cry, my friend added that her sister, whom she had called long distance to tell the news of my joining, would be upset since she understood how happy this had made Linda. My friend added, "If you aren't inter-

ested in doing it for yourself, then do it for me. I am pleading with you." What could I say? I did say I wish I could just be left alone but that I didn't want to hurt her or anyone, so I'd try it. We hung up.

I know Linda needs me as a friend. She likes me and is depending on me to be with her in this class, but it isn't something I will enjoy. And to be very truthful, I don't get much enjoyment from this friendship. Is it my duty to continue? How far should I go? Can I learn to respect myself and my wishes first? Should I let my feelings of resentment cause the friendship to die totally, or just continue to put up with Linda's manipulation?

This type of story is repeated every day in many different forms and in offices, factories, school, churches, homes, and neighborhoods. Feeling people grapple with guilt when they don't do things that others expect, yet they wrestle with resentment when they do things for people that they would rather not do.

Thinkers would respond as Tana's husband did at the very beginning: "If I wasn't interested in taking aerobics, I wouldn't go, no matter who invited me or for what reasons. Friendship is not based on forcing you to do what you don't want to do."

Choosing to Feel Guilty

Actually, sometimes we choose to feel guilty, meaning inadequate or inferior.

One summer on our way home from vacation, Jim dropped me off at my mother's for a week—the first time I had ever visited her without the family. I was excited.

Jim and our two youngest teenagers, who had been with us on the trip, continued on home with a loaded camper. As I envisioned their facing the monotonous challenge of unloading and putting away (a job I usually supervised), going through the stack of mail, answering numerous phone calls with reports from the church field, and getting the household in the swing again, I felt guilty about not being there to help.

When Jim called to let me know they had arrived safely, I confessed, "I really feel guilty about not being there." Jim's reply jolted me. "If you want to feel guilty, go right ahead," he said bluntly. "I'm perfectly happy for you to be where you are."

I decided right then and there that if *he* didn't fault me for not being on hand, then feeling guilty was my own choice. So I should forget it. I did, and I had a wonderful, guilt-free visit.

Resisting Guilt

Just because you feel guilty, inferior, inadequate, or to blame, doesn't mean that you really are. When you understand yourself and appreciate how you have been designed, a lot of people can be unhappy or disappointed with you or critical of your behavior yet you can quietly say to yourself, "They have poor taste." That is not egotism, but just recognizing and preserving self-worth.

When family, friends, or co-workers intentionally or otherwise put unfair expectations on you and you have automatically taken the blame or performed duties just to keep peace, the guilt that you feel must be quelled at the outset if you want to keep resentment from taking root. Brenda illustrates this point with her story:

> Mother expects me to come over every Saturday afternoon. I feel anxious about it, because I know it will be a negative visit. But I feel it is something I *have* to do as a good little daughter who is duty-bound. If I don't go, she gives me trouble.
> "My house needs vacuuming," she'll say casually. Or

"If someone doesn't soon cut this grass, I'll have to get out there myself." Then, for much of the time, I listen to her concerns about the other children as well as how Dad is mistreating her. What do I really want to do? Struggle with guilt? No, I must learn how to handle it, especially since much of what Mom complains about she could take care of easily by hiring it done. She's stingy with money unless she can wear or eat what it buys. And she's not nearly as tied down and mistreated as she makes it sound.

I'm between a rock and a hard place. If I go, I resent the burden. When I think about not going, I'm overcome with not only guilt but also fear. I'm afraid that if I don't go, I'll be talked about and criticized. Somewhere through the years, as the oldest, I have accepted responsibility for protecting Mother from her problems. Or possibly I feel guilty because my husband is so sensitive to my needs and gives me plenty of space.

Perhaps Mother is jealous of my situation. [Here Brenda shows fresh insight.] Who knows? But one thing *I* know is that I'm learning to ask myself questions: "Is this problem mine? Can I prevent it? Could Mom solve this if she wanted to? Am I obligated to visit my mother even though it distresses me? Is it really helping her for me to do her work?"

A statement from an earlier chapter bears repeating at this point. Insisting on harmony at any cost may be short-cutting someone else's growth in responsibility and maturity. Giving in is not always wise.

Some people have been tagged "gluttons for punishment" because in order to get attention, even abusive attention, these poor souls will bend over backward to do for people what they really don't want to do. But they are so hungry for acceptance, they will do anything to get a wee tidbit of approval.

That type of affection is short-lived, however. Many people suffer from "performance love," which demands rule keeping or achievements as a requirement for approval: "If you will do such-and-such, I'll love you." This keeps people psychologically dependent on the "stingy" givers. Another name for this stance is conditional love. (One husband really gets the booby prize for telling his wife, "If you loved me, you would be the way I want you to be.")

When softhearted people feel a little selfish or mean, they are probably wising up. If Feelers never act until they feel right or good about decisions, someone's foot will no doubt be on their neck to get on with it. We cannot blindly trust decisions based solely on feelings.

Brennan Manning, quoting Vincent Bellotta, III in *A Stranger to Self-Hatred,* says something to the effect that powerful "others" will try to make us conform and live up to their expectations. We may have to run the risk of being defiant, of standing up for ourselves, to hold our own against people who have dominance over us. We are called to stand on our own two feet and develop the ability to say yes or no as we make decisions for the governance of our lives. To be seduced from following our own path is to be controlled by others. Being a people pleaser should not require submission to their tyrannical demands.

Shortcutting Your Guilt Trips

Learning Self-Respect

Tana's question, "Can I learn to respect myself first?" provides the answer to all her questions. When you respect yourself, respect from others will occur naturally.

Feeling people, especially, suffer in another way: taking inappropriate blame. "I either caused these problems or could have prevented them," Martha moaned. "What did I do wrong? My daughter is ill and my husband is homosexual."

"We've been married for twenty-five years," Gloria shared. "Every time one of our teenagers stays out too late or has any kind of problem, Phil rakes that kid over the coals but then blames *me* for his or her infraction. Our son questioned his dad recently about why he 'blames Mom' for everything, and that really started an argument. Although I know I'm not a perfect wife or mother, I wonder if everything that goes wrong at home is my fault."

Every problem that surfaces is not one person's fault, and warmhearted people have to learn how to shield themselves from self-condemnation. They must *choose* not to have hurt feelings or guilty regrets.

I used to take the blame for every church squabble, thinking I either caused it or could have squelched it. When it became apparent to me that Jim was not devastated by discord in general, and neither was his self-esteem tied to popularity, I released myself from my false guilt. Jim taught me to ask myself a couple of questions: Is it true that I'm the cause? Am I responsible for what other people say and do?

Dealing with Mixed Emotions

When someone wants or expects you to do something you have neither the time nor inclination to do, how can you deal with the mixed emotions involved? Should you do what the other person wants, thus avoiding a confrontation in which feelings might be hurt or anger generated? Should you make an excuse to get out of it? How about just saying no!

You must be prepared for a struggle with mixed emotions in these circumstances, especially if you are a Feeling person in temperament. When a distasteful expectation is first presented, either ask for time to think it over (if you are not sure what you want) or tell the person right off that the answer is no. This assumes, of course, that you are not dealing with an employer or other person who has the legitimate authority to make this request of you. You may need some privacy to swish around the decision in your thinking chamber before responding, and that's okay. But remember, if you don't say no when that's what you mean, communications get scrambled and resentment creeps in.

Some people would rather stretch the truth and tell a polite lie than risk hurting or angering someone with an honest answer. It goes something like this:

"Want to go to tonight's ball game with me?" teenaged Jack asks his schoolmate Bill.

"Oh, I'm sorry," says Bill—who doesn't want to go because he's been annoyed with Jack all week—"but Dad has made some plans for us that I can't get out of." This indeed stretches the truth, since Bill is just planning to stay home and watch television with his father. Bill feels he needs a more plausible explanation for Jack, believing that if he turns down the invitation outright, the tables may be turned if he wants something from Jack in the future. Besides, Bill wants to stay in good graces with the crowd in which Jack is a popular leader, so he tries a ploy quite handy for young people—he uses parental wishes as an "out."

Using contrived excuses—lying—makes you dislike yourself in the long run. Ask yourself whether it is worth disliking yourself as a person just to avoid having someone else dislike you. Better to like the person you spend the most time with—yourself.

Learn to be honest with yourself and others. Anytime you give a reason why you can't fulfill a request, check to see if it's a false reason just to protect the other person's feelings. Feeling people want the other person to think they *would* comply if they possibly could. But you cannot maintain popularity with everyone all the time without losing respect for yourself.

Some workers allow fellow employees to take advantage of their desire for harmony or friendship by doing favors. When these softhearted people finally wake up to the fact that others have taken advantage of their goodness (willingness to work unpopular overtime slots or do the distasteful jobs), only a painful process of confrontation will change the pattern.

Maintaining Self-Esteem

Unless you respect yourself, no one else will respect you either. Ask yourself the following questions when a request is made of you:

Is it unfair to me?

Will I dislike doing that?

Do I want to say no?

Am I being pressured?

Am I trying to earn someone's approval?

Do I lack respect for the person doing the asking?

If you answer "yes" to most of these questions, someone may be trying to push you in a direction you don't want to go. Don't let it happen!

A person tortured with guilt feelings, inadequacy, inferiority, or the tendency to always take the blame can find relief by memorizing and adopting the following guidelines:

I cannot please everyone all the time.

A request for help doesn't constitute an "assignment" or guarantee that I have the strength, money, or time to comply.

Just because several disagree with me doesn't mean I am wrong.

Harmony is nice, but my efforts won't guarantee it all the time.

I am not put in this world to be popular. If certain others disapprove of me or my style or sometimes think I am selfish, mean, or arrogant, that's *their* problem.

I strongly recommend *Telling Yourself the Truth* by William Backus and Marie Chapian—an excellent guide for teaching Feeling people (and others, too) how to think logically—and honestly.

Resolve your mixed emotions as soon as possible, so that the destructive effects on your identity and beauty are negligible. Guilt can drain the energy of your self-respect as surely as harmful insects suck life-sustaining juices right out of the stems and leaves of plants.

Fighting Depression

Depression is often the result of a poor self-image, which, as we have already seen, can sometimes be caused by unrealistically appropriating feelings of guilt and inadequacy because we have failed to comply with another's expectations. One woman, totally rejected by her new husband's family because she was a divorcée, suffered deep depression for seven years thereafter. Having already experienced twelve years of physical and mental abuse by her alcoholic first husband, this new rejection on top of her past hurt created too much stress.

The alienation from his family caused her husband anxiety as well, which became another source of guilt for the woman. She lost her job because of her inability to function, further intensifying her self-image problem.

When her self-esteem was finally restored through counseling, she was able to shrug off her in-laws' narrowmindedness as their problem, not hers. Her husband— also softhearted—found new confidence and contentment in standing up to his family. This once-unhappy wife has found employment and is now busy helping other depressed women get help.

When some Feeling people are isolated from opportunities to help people, the result is often diagnosed as depression or a spiritual problem. This type of individual just has to have exposure to others to function optimally. The positive feedback they receive from doing nice things for others is their fulfillment for being a person. If a Feeling person is involved in an occupation that is not people-oriented in some way, he or she may suffer extreme unhappiness. Unless there is a chance to help people in off hours, a change of jobs (even one with less pay) might improve their self-image.

An introverted, sensory, softhearted man who preferred a scheduled lifestyle (ISFJ) worked fairly contentedly as a machinist for years, until forced overtime made it impossible to fit in his volunteer prison activities. He became very unhappy, but blamed it on spiritual weakness, midlife crisis, his wife, and so on. When a company layoff forced him to find other work, he returned to a secretarial position he had held before he was married and has been a satisfied man ever since. He needed direct contact with people.

Many Thinking husbands—or sometimes Feeling ones who are possessive—disapprove of their wives' spending fuel, time, and energy in visiting friends or volunteering their services to those in need. One such husband said to his wife when she wanted to reach out to a family who suffered a fire, "I'll tell you when and whom to help. If you have time on your hands, learn to sew or do something more around the house." This woman suffered deep depression and even physical ailments until she got involved in serving others who would respond with appreciation.

When our self-worth hinges totally on others' acceptance, opinions, and positive feedback, we are at their mercy. But there is a legitimate, instinctive need for Feeling people to locate satisfying sources of approval.

The latest research indicates that depression can be alleviated by well-chosen behavior therapy as well as by medicine. My own informal research bears this out. "Walk and talk" are my suggestions. Exercise is wonderful therapy for cleansing the mind and body, and talking is a natural way to unload bulging bags of depressed feelings.

"Healthy" Guilt

One dictionary definition of guilt is: "The fact of being responsible for an offense or wrongdoing; breaking the law; remorseful awareness of having done something wrong."

Real guilt is serious business. In no way do I want to dilute one's responsibility for accepting appropriate blame for wrongdoing. This type of guilt cannot be explained away. Honest confession and restitution, if possible, is the only way to rid oneself of true guilt.

Many children lie because they want to avoid their parents' wrath. They find that their inner guilt about lying is easier to bear than the parental uproar and rehearsal of their infraction. (Isn't it true that we adults also stretch or avoid the truth in order to save our reputation or admit that we are to blame?)

I like the illustration of a mother who finds her little boy's broken car behind the couch. If she asks, "Johnny, where is your new car?" she's likely to force Johnny into a lying "I don't know" in order to avoid a bawling out or spanking. It is a good psychological principle not to ask questions if you know the answer. If the mother says instead, "Johnny, I found your new little car today. I'm so sorry it's broken," Johnny is likely to say, "Yeah, I tried to ride it and I was too heavy."

Many children complain that adults do not give them time to give their side of the story. Parents can encourage truthfulness by calmly hearing the child's version and fitting the punishment with the offense. (This, too, is a subject for another book.)

Real guilt indicates the presence of sin. But John 1:9 promises: "If we confess our sins, [God] is faithful and just and will forgive us our sins and purify us from all unrighteousness." We must all learn to appreciate good, "healthy" guilt, which reminds us of our innate selfishness and unconcern. As Scott Peck reminds us in *The Road Less Travelled,* we must learn to listen to our consciences. A fascinating chapter.

Though I would not advocate ignoring legitimate guilt feelings, I do suggest a form of release for overly sensitive people who are unhealthily controlled by false guilt. They must learn to consult logic in order to protect themselves from both self-punishment and the agony of being falsely accused. For example, even though Feeling people are naturally sensitive and make personal sacrifices easily, they are quite capable of being very ugly, selfish, and unconcerned about the needs or feelings of others, especially when they have suffered much personal hurt, neglect, and rejection themselves. After therapeutic healing through positive communication that assures them of their intrinsic value and raises their self-esteem, healthy guilt can bring about a realization of their true selves.

"Healthy" guilt-handling for a Thinker would include purposely considering the emotional needs and sensitivity of the other 50 percent of the population. Just as Vincent Bellotta also projected, failure to assume responsibility for the direction of our lives and that of others and neglecting to promote love, in light of God's design for us, *should* engender guilt.

We can learn valuable lessons from a flower garden. Only as we recognize the higher order of our creation "in God's image," do we come to know our strengths and weak-

nesses and those of others. Then we will wisely adjust our expectations of ourselves and our fellow humans so that the best harmony can be realized. Much heartache can be avoided if we work together to rid God's garden of the destructive insects of guilt.

5

Resentments— The Weeds of Disharmony

Whoever of you loves life and desires to see many good days, keep your tongue from evil and your lips from speaking lies. Turn from evil and do good; seek peace and pursue it. Psalm 34:12–14

Weeds are always unwelcome in a garden. A flower garden overtaken by weeds is a hideous sight and usually indicates gross neglect. Even a few weeds can spoil the intended beauty and harmony.

Most gardeners agree that weeds will flourish despite adverse circumstances. Most are tough, thorny, and very difficult to destroy. If left to mature, weeds ripen, producing thousands more of their highly productive seeds.

Resentments resemble weeds in many ways, sprouting when conditions are right, cropping up overnight, and surviving with no encouragement. At first they are small and inconspicuous. Ignored, they mature and rear their ugly heads unexpectedly. In no time, resentments can destroy a beautiful life. As with weeds, the seeds of resentment can live buried for many years before germinating. Complex resentments must be dug up by the roots in order to be thoroughly destroyed.

The Origin of Resentments

According to one dictionary, resentment is "a feeling of indignant displeasure at something regarded as a wrong, insult, or injury." In other words, it is a result of a real or imagined offense.

Resentments germinate mainly from unfulfilled expectations. As discussed in the previous two chapters, people sometimes resent themselves for not reaching their goals or for failing to please others. At other times, unfulfilled expectations—both assumed and spoken—that we have put on other people sprout into resentments on both sides.

Resentments can spring from job terminations, unkept promises, oversights, passive attitudes, lack of recognition, disrespect, unfair treatment, negligence, irresponsibilities, laziness, failure to assist, pushiness, presumptuous behavior, lack of understanding, personal defaults of all kinds. The list is endless. Many deeply rooted resentments stem from long-ago emotional or physical abuse, causing mental disorders that usually require professional assistance to remove.

Weeding Out Resentments

Resentments are relatively easy to pull while they are young and so tiny they are noticed only upon close inspection. Sensitive people unwittingly nurture their growth because the only way most Feelers know they are okay is by the way others treat them.

Softhearted people, for example, usually speak the way they would like to be spoken to—tenderly:

"I'm sorry, but I have to disagree." Or "I realize that this is a great imposition but. . . ." They resent not receiving reprimands, disagreements, and directions in the same manner, since otherwise they register them as put-downs.

Similarly, Feeling people also resent not being consulted in decision making, as Julie explained: "When my husband announced that he was offering our home to his teenaged niece without first asking my opinion, I was irate."

When I interviewed her husband, Dean, about this, he said, "Julie complains no matter what I do, so I decided I might as well do what I thought was right. The girl needs a home."

"Julie probably resists your decisions because she's not sure about her importance," I suggested. "Do you tell her how important she is to you? That she's Number One?"

"I don't talk like that!" he stormed. "In fact, we can't seem to talk."

"Unless you acknowledge her style of listening, and learn to speak her language, you'll have two crises on your hands," I said. "If Julie feels manipulated and taken for granted, she'll not be willing to help your niece, which may likely intensify problems for all concerned."

Many weeks later, Julie expressed some honest evaluations and mature solutions in a letter to her husband:

> Dear Dean: Do you see how my keeping my thoughts inside angered you? This is how I feel when I discover your hidden "I resent"s. Why can't we expose these resentments as they develop and avoid the two-hour pot luck?
>
> I want to encourage you to become the best person you can become. I want you to encourage me to become the best person I can become. I long to be totally honest. I yearn for you to be the same. I will remove my expectations of wanting to be verbally affirmed. When it happens, it will be a bonus.
>
> When I feel you are allowing situations to supersede my importance, I'll try to deal tactfully with it. Let's start over. Old hurts can't be solved nor even recalled properly. . . .

Many resentments, especially those originating in the home, appear trivial to bystanders, but these little weeds quickly grow into big ones if they are ignored. After many years of growth, they will have to be painfully dug out by the roots, since plowing under does not destroy their seeds of disharmony.

Eliminating Young Resentments

In the Home

Example 1. "My wife is certainly not keeping her end of the bargain," Ryan ranted. "Our house just doesn't look like a home. Not a plant in sight. My mom had plants in every room."

Saying "I do" does not automatically endow a wife with a green thumb, any more than it equips a husband to repair the washing machine. Ryan's expectations are unfair.

Example 2. "What are you going to cook for my parents, Alice?"

"I've told you, Alvin, that I can't cook. You've certainly observed that over the last few months. I've done nothing to indicate that I would ever be able to cook," she defended.

"You're a woman! Some little part of me still secretly hoped you could cook," he pouted.

Some Intuitive women neither like to cook nor enjoy taking care of plants. Many resent cleaning a house and washing clothes. Since they prefer analytical involvements, they often enjoy rearing children, which involves future planning and different kinds of growth—psychological, emotional, spiritual, and physical. In a home, an individual's expectations must be analyzed carefully and blended with the temperamental inclinations of others in the family.

A mother who works outside the home may resent other members of the family not helping with household chores. In my own experience, I like to be in charge of the house until time pressures intervene. Then I expect help, especially if someone is merely watching TV or reading a magazine. I have accepted housecleaning as my responsibility since I elected to get married and have children. Even though I'm an Intuitive, I actually enjoy housework. But cleaning the tub is one job I dislike, so I have tried to dump this chore.

Several times, when Roger was living here after college, I mentioned that the tub needed to be cleaned, that I didn't have time to clean it, that he helped dirty it. Because I dislike the job and because he pays room and board, I felt a bit guilty about trying to slough it off on him, so I hoped he would volunteer out of sympathy for me. My effort was useless. Thinkers (like Roger) are fairly guilt-trip immune.

I put the Ajax can and the cleaning cloth on the tub. No luck. Once I sprinkled the cleansing powder in the tub before he showered, but he didn't take that hint either. But my thinking that I deserved this kind of assistance without asking created the right expectation condition for resentment to build up. I didn't want to resent Roger, so I applied two helpful rules: (1) mentally acknowledge the expectation (or resentment), and (2) substitute a verbalized request or desire for the unspoken or unclear expectation. It went like this:

"Roger, I'd like you to take a couple of minutes to clean the tub this morning." This provided him with a choice— yes or no. I could learn immediately what his response would be rather than wonder if he caught the hint.

"No problem," he replied. As easy as that! Was I ever impressed. If he had said no, we would have had reason for a family conference. A person who respects and loves you will want you to be satisfied. If your requests are unreasonable, it's better to get that out in the open.

I have discovered that resentment revolves around things one usually dislikes doing and/or is expected to do. Many parents feel guilty if they fail to meet the physical and emotional needs of their family, especially if they are single parents. People can even feel guilty for feeling

guilty! On top of that, the guilt may be tinged with resentment when they receive no positive responses from
their children, who are often too young or immature to
appreciate sacrifices made for them.

"I used to make meals and other things to get approval
from my family," Celia confessed. "But when they didn't
come through with appreciation and a little assistance, I
was filled with resentment and self-pity. I hate resenting
the people I love the most," she sighed.

Celia did not realize that it is unfair to expect a spouse
or child to be thoughtful in the same areas and ways that
she was. But anyone can learn to be sensitive to specific
needs once they understand how important it is to a person that they care about.

After Celia pinpointed the source of her resentment and
expressed her expectations to herself, she reported: "I decided that doing my duties because I *wanted* to would
bypass my resentment build-up. I have discovered that
when I don't expect appreciation, and then do receive some,
it's a precious gift. My resentment toward my family has
subsided greatly, now that I don't expect something they
won't or don't know how to give. I feel much better now."

Most family members are unaware how much for
granted they take their moms and dads and need to be
reminded from time to time that appreciation is in vogue.
It's even all right for a mom to say, "I'm getting breakfast
because I want to, but I could surely use some applause
about now!"

A wife may resent her softhearted husband's tendency
to let his boss and relatives push him around and take
advantage of his need for harmony. But a bossy wife creates a fertile ground for resentment to grow in him and
in the children who are listening. (This will be discussed
more fully in chapter 7.)

Sometimes parents resent a child for deeper reasons, as
in the following account from Elaine:

My husband and I are separated. Lisa, our daughter, blames me for her father's inability to present a firm backbone for this family. I have accepted all her accusations because I feel very inadequate, as well as wanting to keep peace—even if it means taking the blame for something not totally my fault.

However, when I see Lisa walking up the driveway with Susie, expecting me to baby-sit, I actually seethe with resentment. All she wants is what I can do for her. She cares nothing about how much she imposes or what kind of mess her child makes in my house or whether I'm tired.

I counseled Elaine to apply the twofold approach I had used with Roger in the tub-scrubbing incident:

1. *Acknowledge the source of resentment mentally.* "Lisa expects me to take the blame for our separation. I am not responsible for her father's actions and inabilities. Lisa expects me to take care of Susie without forewarning. She expects me to meet her needs but cares nothing about mine."

2. *Verbalize the expectation.* "Lisa, I would prefer to keep Susie when it suits me, rather than any time *you* choose." (This declaration calls for a response from Lisa. They will both need to communicate about reasonable expectations. Elaine might start off by saying, "Are you aware that I also hurt over this separation and expect a little kindness, support, and consideration from you?" An answer is requested.)

In the Office

In an office where workers share duties, resentment often runs rampant as each expects the others to do those jobs that no one likes to do. Jenny had this to say:

The other gals assume I like to answer the phone, just because I can't stand to hear it ring and I don't want the boss to bawl us out. They also just walk out at the end of the day as though I'm supposed to lock up everything, clean out the coffee pot, and turn off the machines. I guess I have just chosen to do these jobs to keep peace, but inside I'm burning.

Even though our boss has never told me to do all those extra jobs—I just accepted doing them without complaint—to stop doing them now would probably cause some friction within the office. They suppose I am only doing those things because I enjoy it, but I really have deep resentment toward them all.

Jenny needs to apply the second part of our rule—verbalize the expectations—so she might tell her co-workers, "Answering the phone is not just *my* responsibility, so I would like one of you to answer it, too. And I want us to take turns locking up, cleaning up, and turning off machines."

The others' responses to each of these statements will provide opportunity for good communication and clear the air. If not, the boss certainly needs to set some guidelines.

Of course, turning expectations into requests could be answered with "I don't care what you want" or "I can't deliver what you request." There are risks involved in being honest. But I would rather know, for instance, that Roger doesn't care how I feel about cleaning the tub and never intends to clean it, than keep hoping that sometime he will appreciate me enough to do it without being asked.

In the Community

Monica was nearly ecstatic about having an entire week to herself—the first time in her thirteen years as a mother. Jennifer was finally old enough to join her brother and sister for the YMCA day camp. Monica was pleased with her ability to make such a big decision without the help of her husband. But then Mrs. Strong called about the opportunity to be a counselor, promising that "your children would get to go free." That didn't really influence

Monica, but she was filled with parental guilt when Mrs. Strong said, "Most parents don't realize how much they miss by not being with their children in such a creative outdoor atmosphere. And we are desperate for help."

"There's no reason why I couldn't go," Monica reasoned aloud. "I really didn't have anything definite planned except to read and do some writing and maybe shop alone." *It's selfish of me to want a whole week without my children,* she thought, which raised her guilt level by several decibels. *And I just might miss something important to my children,* she further counseled herself.

"I need to know your decision right away," Mrs. Strong coaxed.

"Okay, I'll do it," Monica said.

"As soon as I hung up," Monica told me later, "I knew I had made the wrong decision, but I had been trying to make Thinking decisions and stick with them, so I figured this was one I'd have to stick to.

"I dreaded each day at camp. I was bored and kept thinking about how much I'd looked forward to my private time. I made the most of the week by enjoying the out-of-doors and getting acquainted with the other counselors and leaders. But I still regret letting Mrs. Strong talk me into something I really didn't want to do. I don't know if I resent myself or Mrs. Strong the most. It's my Feeling nature in charge of me again," she analyzed correctly. "How can I control this tendency?"

Those who base their decisions on feelings are most often guilty of saying yes when they mean no. As previously mentioned, they are wise to make a pact with themselves to automatically say, "I need time to think it over," to anyone who wants them to be on a committee, teach a class, donate a day, be in a club, volunteer to do anything, and so on. If the other person presses for an immediate answer, let it be "No."

As you later consider the request, first ask yourself: "Is this something I really *want* to do?" Then apply the technique of a Thinking decision-maker by writing down the pros and cons of doing or not doing it. As you expose new facts and possibilities, run the options through a Thinker's head, if this is feasible.

Meeting thorny resentments head-on takes courage, especially for Feeling people, who want to be helpful and need approval from those around them. The positive side is that disagreements provide material for discussion. Solving little problems forms invisible bonds between people of all temperaments.

Unfulfilled expectations, which create the climate for the weeds of resentment to grow, look very harmless in their infancy. But unless we conscientiously and consistently remove these young sprouts, our garden's beauty will be under attack.

Yanking Out Mature Resentments

Resentments with a few years' growth are not so easily eliminated. They must be yanked out forcibly, though taking action at this juncture will likely disturb other plants around them. That's a risk we must take if we envision an attractive garden.

In the Home

Juanita tells of her longstanding resentment, which centers on her in-laws' expectations:

> We live with my husband's father; rather he lives with us. We're the only ones who still live in his hometown. This works okay until the holidays, when Wayne's brothers and their families descend on us from out of town to visit Grandpa. Then my resentment really builds up.
>
> Every one of our holidays is pre-planned. I'm cooking, cleaning, and crowding up rather than spending the vacation time with our children. I'm an elementary-school teacher. We never get to do what we as a family would enjoy.
>
> I resent terribly not being able to establish our own family tradition with our four children, who are fast approaching high school. Wayne feels the same way that I do, but we don't know how we can swing private time with all his family here. We'd love to celebrate Christmas with just our children, or sometimes with *my* family.
>
> We've considered going out to eat, but then I would feel guilty about not hostessing. Besides that, Wayne's family wouldn't understand and would be hurt, which would give us another problem to solve. Wayne just does not have the courage to confront his family, but we agree something has to be done.
>
> We've hinted about having Christmas somewhere else, but we really don't want to leave home, especially since we're the only ones with young children. I don't know why they don't invite their father to their homes. They've all had children, so they should know how important spending time with them is. But they've done this now for several years, and I don't think it's a rut they want to leave. We're trapped.

Family expectations hold millions in their silent grip. The resentment they activate can grow like a blight, ultimately disfiguring or destroying healthy relationships.

"Which do you think is more detrimental," I asked Juanita, "your resentment or their hurt? You are not only upset with them because they come, but you are disappointed with yourself for not having the courage to schedule your own family time. So you end up with two mads.

"Wayne's relatives have their private family time all the other weeks of the year. You are never alone, unless you purposely plan things away from home. His family has placed expectations on you to be present because they have no idea you'd rather do something else.

"Resentment ends in defeat, so what you're piling up will eventually surface and produce a big hurt. Better to remove resentments while they're manageable than to undergo a major upheaval. When something unexpected or undesirable happens, a willingness to confront exactly what you're feeling gives you some measure of control."

"But I'd feel guilty if it hurt anyone's feelings," Juanita predicted.

"Would you rather ignore the problem and feel resentful or feel guilty but be working toward a solution? Doing the right thing doesn't always feel right."

"You're right, I've got to face the music. Oh, I hate confrontation with a passion," she moaned.

"Yes, you probably will suffer from guilt, but you must tell yourself the truth—that having a private family affair, the desire of your heart, is not sinful. And that resenting someone who stands in the way is.

"Just because you feel guilty doesn't mean you necessarily are. Make sure your intentions are noble. You are not trying to avoid people or shirk your duty, just attempting to establish family traditions the way you and Wayne envision them. If you let the years tick away much longer and never satisfy your desire—fulfill your needs—the roots of your resentment toward your father-in-law and perhaps Wayne and his entire family will extend even deeper.

"Begin looking for the positives in this event. Make a commitment to meet the challenge in a way that makes you a stronger person. It takes a disciplined effort to learn to say, 'It's up to me to make something good come out of this.' Maybe the out-of-town family would actually enjoy having Grandpa visit them if they only knew you wouldn't mind sharing him at holidays. Wayne's family may even feel that you monopolize Grandpa. They may also assume that you approve of the family tradition of coming to your house.

"In any case, Wayne should not only be present for the discussion; he should lead it. His family would no doubt accept his opinions with less resentment than they would yours."

Airing their difficulties was not as painful as Juanita had anticipated. When Wayne's brothers and sisters heard the facts, they were quite willing to make adjustments. Each family has chosen a holiday to share with Grandpa, who really enjoys a change of scenery. Juanita and Wayne have even more freedom than they had hoped.

These same principles can be applied to the office, school, community, and church. Old resentments will not go away without a weeding effort. It may be helpful at this point to mention that Structured people are usually more willing than their Spontaneous counterparts to plod through problems step by step.

Many Sensing-Feeling-Spontaneous people (SFP) practice the ostrich method of sticking their heads in the sand and expecting the problems to disappear. They don't. They just spread.

Intuitives are generally more likely to tackle relationship problems, because past failures do not discourage them. But Feeling-Intuitives may avoid confrontations as long as possible since they do not like to disrupt "harmony," which to them means the absence of argument. We know that silence is no guarantee that harmony is present. Better to cause a little trouble to clear up resentments when they start than allow a blight of destructive uncontrolled growth.

Uprooting Ancient Resentments

Molly, a young mother of two, harbored a resentment so filled with pain that she buried its memory deeply and had never told anyone about it. Her father had told her as a child that she was God's gift to him and that she should never reveal their secrets. This father sexually abused his daughter for years before she realized what was happening. When Molly finally understood that it was wrong and began resisting his overtures, he would force her into compliance. When she threatened to tell her mother, he countered with "I'll leave. Who'll take care of your brothers and sisters, then?" Guilt and fear gripped her for three years. (At the same time her dad was taking advantage of Molly, he was being honored as Father of the Year by his church.)

Molly finally left home by getting married. But she worried about her little sisters, especially since she had never told anyone about her father—not even her mother. (Records show that most wives deny that incestuous abuse could be true and choose to reject the daughter.) Molly hoped she could forget what happened to her, but instead her resentment toward her father intensified.

Several years elapsed. Though Molly avoided her father as much as possible, guilt, fear, and resentment were taking their toll on her. Molly's relationship with her husband was adversely affected. And now that they had a baby girl, she was not comfortable bringing her around her father. Fear for her daughter's well-being is what brought Molly for professional help, which was also needed to heal her own emotional wounds.

Many, many mothers voice this concern. Many times it involves fear of a brother or uncle. Sexual abuse is one of the most serious problems that a person faces, and it *has* to be dealt with. Molly needs to share her information with her sisters and mother in order to protect the other little girls. Of course, any person who physically abuses a child needs psychological counseling. No doubt, her father is victim to his own deep-rooted resentments and unfulfilled expectations, which need professional attention.

Uprooting this fearful resentment will certainly create problems for the entire family, but in the long run it will eliminate much of its deep-seated pain and prevent worse consequences in the future. Such ancient resentments have to be carefully dug out by their well-established roots, as the following also illustrates:

Joel was born to Shirley while she was in high school, and her mother made sure that Shirley suffered emotionally for getting pregnant. Shirley had unsuccessfully attempted to gain her mother's approval since childhood, but her unfulfilled expectations kept Shirley's self-esteem at zero.

Shirley finally moved out on her own, accepting the struggles of single parenting. For years she worked long, exhausting hours doing work that didn't interest her just for the check that would support Joel and herself. *At least my son will appreciate and approve of me,* she reasoned. However, even that expectation backfired when Joel moved out the day after he graduated from high school. Shirley had expected that—out of gratitude for all she had sacrificed for him—he would stay and take care of her, now that he was an adult.

Joel's top priority was obviously not his mother's welfare. Often a parent like Shirley is filled with resentment toward anyone who receives her child's affection and attention (which is most often the child's spouse). In her case, the pain went deeper, since she had years ago been disappointed by her own parent.

Expecting grown children to stick around to offer support as well as company is a source of great disappointment for possessive parents. Young people expect that they have earned freedom to launch out on their own pursuits and enter their private world of relationships. Parents are better advised to look way ahead, anticipate the time when their children will probably leave, and encourage them to be independent, even though that means being left alone. A parent's sacrificial years with a child should not create an expectation that obligates the child.

Naomi's story provides one more illustration and a solution:

> My mother has made all my decisions since I was a child. She chose my hairstyle, my friends, my school courses, my clothing, my summer jobs—everything. If I ever disagreed with her opinion, she knew how to put a guilt trip on me. My, the guilt!
>
> Mother wanted me to equate her authority with God's. Down deep I knew I should insist on making some of my own decisions, but no one crossed Mom at our house, not even our father. He just sat back quietly and let her have control. My way of rebelling was to marry someone she did not approve of. I didn't really approve of Ned either, but it felt good to go against my mother's wishes for once. I also wanted an excuse to leave home.
>
> I have paid for my mistake many times over. My biggest problem now is a poor marriage, but I still detest my mother's trying to dictate my decisions. I hate myself for being pushed around.

Like Naomi, many people reject themselves if they feel rejected by someone they love. But Naomi also harbored a very strong case of resentment against her mother. Being honest was difficult for Naomi because the unjustified guilt she felt for not receiving her mother's approval was a difficult pill to swallow. Holding long-term resentment means you have given that other person control of your emotional state. Naomi had never learned that her own self-image was as important as recognizing others' worth. Naomi would never recover her self-esteem until she got rid of the burden of her resentment.

Naomi had waited expectantly for years for her mother to improve and become what she wanted in a parent. She now knew that there was no way to change her mother. Her mother was "real" the way she was. Like many other Introverts (especially if they are Intuitives and Spontaneous problem solvers), Naomi had tried to change the situation by avoiding a confrontation. She had curtailed visits with her mother, but that injured her father and her children and failed to get at the roots of the problem. The only option left was to change her own attitude, which meant forgiving her mother.

Naomi did not want to confront her mother with a lifetime list of resentments which her mother would probably deny anyway, so she rehearsed her resentments to an empty chair in which she envisioned her mother sitting.

"My mother has changed," Naomi announced at our next session.

"Have you talked with her in person about your resentments?" I questioned.

"No, I haven't. That's what's so weird," she said. "Mom doesn't know anything about that list. I saw her briefly the other night. For once she asked no questions. But she told my grandparents that she has confidence in whatever decision I'm going to make regarding my marriage.

"But best of all, I feel peace for the first time in years. I have recently learned that my mother disappointed her mother when she got married. She's had problems similar to mine without my knowing it. She was trying to force me to avoid the same problems she had had as a young girl. I have to appreciate her for that," Naomi said with a heavy sigh.

To keep her resentments under control, Naomi should do only those things that she wants to do, even if her mother suggests otherwise. Honestly acknowledging her differences in opinion with her mother will also ward off new resentments.

In the Scripture ". . . the truth will set you free" (John 8:32), Jesus refers to himself as "the truth." But being honest and truthful in relationship matters also brings another kind of peace. Being honest despite the possibility that others may disapprove, be disappointed, or even outraged is far better than cultivating resentments. Naomi accepted her mother as she was and did not expect change. She could understand why they had differences once she learned that she herself was an Introverted-Intuitive-Spontaneous person while her mother—an Extravert who was also Sensing and highly Structured—was very rule-oriented. Naomi has also lowered her expectations to those her mother could fulfill and has learned to verbally disagree with her mother. Now, though she never expects her mother to agree with her or compliment her on anything, when her mother does bestow approval Naomi considers it an extra treat.

The solution to deeply rooted resentments involves first acknowledging or listing all of one's long-term unfulfilled expectations or offenses. The victim must then forgive the offender, whether or not that person is present or even aware of the injury. The offended one absorbs the hurt of the offender, thus releasing the offender from responsibility.

Lower your expectations of those people who are evidently not temperamentally capable of acting maturely or unselfishly by *your* standards. Some very nice people are insensitive to others' feelings, need for approval, or style of living. Being honest in verbalizing what you want to do or have happen is part of effective communication, which is serious business and not always pleasant, especially at the start.

6

Constructive Anger—
Protective Spraying

*A fool shows his annoyance at once, but a
prudent man overlooks an insult.* Proverbs 12:16

*In your anger do not sin; when you are on your
beds, search your hearts and be silent.* Psalm 4:4

Anger, when properly understood and controlled, can
be a helpful emotion that is beneficial to relationships,
just as insecticides and herbicides are handy remedies for
controlling the insects that chomp on the leaves and stems
of plants or the pesky weeds that slowly strangle tender
root systems. When sprayed or dusted with the right for-
mula, a garden's beauty can be preserved and enhanced.
Inappropriate chemicals or using them at the wrong time
or in incorrect proportions can injure the very plants we
wish to protect.

Expressions of anger are as varied as the weeds and
injurious insects that must be controlled if our garden is
to thrive. Because feelings of anger and how to utilize
them constructively are so widely misunderstood and unappreciated, proper attention must be directed to this
powerful emotion. Uncontrolled or stored anger causes
fears, guilt, embarrassment, hurt, anxieties, or disappoint-

111

ments. Any of these feelings can result in resentment, which is always self-defeating, as we have seen in the previous chapter.

Our basic goal should be to neutralize or prevent common resentments. Developing a positive approach toward anger and learning how to use it properly will accomplish this, since angry feelings slow down our productivity and cloud our thinking. Most of all, out-of-control anger inhibits effective communication.

Misused anger is a giant wrecking ball. It smashes relationships and spreads havoc in the lives of the innocent as well as the offender. The results of misdirected anger are especially deadly when they injure the very people we love the most.

The presence of anger is often a subtle surpriser, surfacing when one least expects it or when time to settle an issue is at a premium. Angry feelings need to be carefully analyzed and followed to their source, but first we need a definition. One dictionary says that anger is "a feeling of extreme displeasure, hostility, indignation, or exasperation toward someone or something; rage; wrath; ire." *Anger* is a general term used to denote temporary displeasure and may have no outward expression. *Rage* and *fury* imply intense, uncontained, explosive emotion. *Fury* can be

very destructive, and *rage* more justified by circumstances. *Ire* is a poetic term for anger, while *resentment* refers to the ill will and suppressed anger generated by a sense of grievance. One feels *indignation* at seeing the mistreatment of someone or something dear and worthy.

Anger Quiz

How much do you really understand about anger? Take the following quiz by circling T (True) or F (False) for each statement. Then check your answers by referring to the key below.

1. The more you love someone, the less you will get angry with that person.   T F
2. Lack of anger and patience are the same.   T F
3. Anger is sin.   T F
4. Anger is a God-given release.   T F
5. Verbally expressing anger is wrong.   T F
6. Unexpressed anger can make you ill.   T F
7. People express anger in different ways.   T F
8. A person chooses whether to be angry.   T F
9. Anger is handled best when ignored.   T F
10. Some people never get angry.   T F
11. Lack of anger could indicate lack of love for the person who has offended you.   T F
12. Letting anger out gradually is better than holding it in.   T F

(*False*: 1–3, 5, 9, 10; *True*: 4, 6–8, 11, 12)

The Sources and Functions of Anger

Many people deny that they have angry feelings because they believe that anger is unspiritual and a sign of immaturity or weakness. Others assume that an aggressive display of temper is the only way anger is expressed or experienced. But anger is evoked when anything or anybody hinders our forward progress, challenges our intelligence, or takes us for granted. In short, we become angry when we are treated with "disrespect." A few common examples:

Mothers' anger is aroused when kids sass them, track in mud, or fail to pick up belongings.

Fathers' anger erupts when offspring lack respect for their authority and fail to consider consequences of an action.

Teachers exhibit anger when students disrupt the class.

Drivers steam when an approaching vehicle's lights are not dimmed or someone tailgates them.

Truckers boil when a slow-moving motorist pulls in front on a steep downgrade.

Children seethe when not allowed to tell their side of the story or when they are yelled at for no apparent reason.

Bosses fume when workers cannot get along or time is wasted.

Wives object to being neglected or taken for granted.

Husbands are offended when not consulted on family decisions.

Lovers' anger is expressed in jealousies.

Anger is functional—a facilitator—appearing in all sorts of styles to alert, warn, or announce existing or approaching problems. Similar to environmental warnings— the nagging buzz of an alarm clock; annoying beepers that summon; buzzers signaling an unbalanced load; whistles, sirens, bells, yells, screams, cries; fire and burglar alarms; the ding-ding-ding at railroad crossings; the silent warnings of blinking lights; the flapping of high-wind pennants; or the signaling of waving flags—a surge of anger is merely a warning that trouble is lurking or already upon us. Immediate attention is critical for making adjustments that will prevent problems, surmount obstacles, or avoid disaster.

Although warnings are annoying, they have a good purpose. Many people either avoid warning signals until they become insensitive to them, or else they become embroiled with the signals themselves, rather than giving attention to the conditions that triggered the alert. It can be risky business to ignore or deal impulsively with feelings of anger. In either case, personal relationships are sure to suffer. Conversely, if anger pinpoints the source of the problem by initiating in-depth communication, sturdy bonds of friendship and love are most likely to develop.

Check the following list to see how many potential sources of anger you perceive in others or regularly experience yourself:

Strong disagreement with room- or house-mates, including one's family

Anguish of inferiority feelings

Hurt from false accusations and put-downs

Distress when taken for granted

Disappointment with others' oversights of your needs

Anxiety stemming from loneliness

Guilt from disagreement with and/or disappointing others

Discouragement with personal failures and lack of initiative

Jealousy and envy of those who receive or achieve abundantly

Pain from neglect

Trauma of physical or mental abuse.

Dissatisfaction with personal appearance or abilities

Many people deny that they ever succumb to feelings of anger—just as many believe that putting their heads in the sand or turning a deaf ear to unpleasantness erases the emotion as well as eliminates the need for resolving the problem. Wrong both times! Angers do not dissolve or dissipate automatically. They either fester from neglect or are acknowledged and handled constructively.

Identifying Anger

Common indications that angry feelings are being expressed include the following behavior symptoms. (Put a check by your favorites, but please don't assume that whenever these problems occur—especially the last six items —angry feelings are definitely the cause.)

grit teeth	cuss, name-call
run away	obscene gesture
bite nails	clench/shake fist
kick, sock	stick out tongue
lie, cry	clammy hands
pull hair	blush, pout
throw things	muscle aches
seethe silently	headache
break something	sleepiness
spit, bite	insomnia
scream, stomp	perspire profusely
slam doors	nausea

Though reading over the list at this calm time may be rather amusing, these expressions can serve as important warnings that an existing or potential problem is threatening our self-esteem or relationship with another person. Unless we give proper attention to anger signals, we will store such a crop of cautions that we will either be overwhelmed and overtaken by their effect or become numbed and insensitive to their message.

When we learn to identify our personal anger signs, whether expressed in explosive outbursts or felt in silent misery, we will better understand ourselves and be able to avoid immature behavior, which never solves anything.

Appreciating Anger

Many strange ideas about feelings of anger exist. For example, some assume that a certain threshold of distress tolerance is present in one's genetic makeup and thus that the inability to cope with problems calmly (or at all) is inherited: "I explode because my dad does." Or "Fury is a family trait." This theory would also imply that it is impossible to change one's reactions and responses permanently.

While there may not be a clear-cut case for a genetic explanation of one's anger threshold, understanding the different temperaments sheds much light on why and how individuals respond and react to stresses. Generally, Extraverts will be verbal when pressured, while Introverts will more likely retreat. Structured people want things settled *now* (especially if they are also Thinkers), but if they are Feelers, they will want someone else to work through the situation.

Feeling people seem to experience the majority of relationship difficulties because they have difficulty functioning without acceptance and harmony. Spontaneous people seem to have the shortest fuses and are more likely to resort to an immediate fight-or-flight technique.

Understand that every temperament, if put under enough stress, is capable of running or fighting, whether the latter recourse be with mouth, fists, or pen. (Several of my clients have shared some stinging letters of angry rebuke that they have had to work through.) We would all be wise not only to appreciate the particular tendencies of each temperament group but endeavor to develop the areas of our own least preferred behavior for better balance.

The few who believe that to admit anger is to be non-spiritual, immature, weak, and totally negative often attempt to conceal their feelings in order to gain both self-respect and others' approval. Ironically, though, heaping guilt on yourself because of your angers produces more subtle hostility. Ignored angers eventually take their toll mentally and physically on others and yourself.

Some mistakenly assume that resignation and passivity are the opposites of anger and thus more acceptable. Others, who cannot silence their feelings, fault themselves for their defensive fly-off-the-handle tendencies. Both of these attitudes are shortsighted and can be dangerously deceptive. Anger itself is neither wrong nor negative. It is simply an attitude, a feeling that gauges something deep inside. How one expresses and handles the emotion is the important thing.

Since so many people assume that to admit anger is to acknowledge their own selfishness, conceit, or weakness, and that showing anger indicates a lack of forgiveness and a moral failure, they may miss the true value of anger as a relational tool.

Anger—what calls it forth and how we acknowledge its existence—is a remarkable revealer of true character. Anger exposes commendable as well as selfish traits, both good and poor values. It is a truism that how we handle an emotional crisis shows our real selves.

A person might plead in embarrassment, "How can I get rid of my temper?" The answer is that you can't, nor would you want to! Anger is here to stay. Anger is one of

God's gifts, and we would be spineless and uninteresting without it.

Handling Anger

Anger, like love, is a feeling all mankind struggles to understand, but the mark of maturity is proven by the way angry feelings are handled. There seem to be two basic *immature* responses to anger—noisy overreaction or stony silence. As already stated, depending on your personality makeup, your expression of anger will usually be either straightforward or disguised. Both are deadly if not appreciated and handled constructively.

Spontaneous and Impulsive Anger

This is the most common or best-known anger response because it is noisy and showy—black eyes and arguments. It also requires the least thought. Some people pop off like firecrackers, curtly speak their minds, or jump to some handy defense with little thought concerning their listener.

Sharp-tongued, outspoken people do benefit somewhat from the pop-off-valve emotional release that comes from venting their feelings, but their relief is often at the expense of others' injured emotions and bodies. Many dislike themselves afterwards, whereas timid people—the sometimes-shy Extraverts or reserved Introverts—may observe the confidence and courage shown and wish that they could stand up and likewise unload their minds.

Since uncontrolled anger of any kind wrecks friendships and confuses issues, outgoing and Spontaneous-Extraverts (who seem to wrestle most with this noisy, impulsive expression of feeling) need to *learn* how to activate the cooling-down system and generate good results.

Ignored or Simmering Anger

Common, too, but rarely called "anger" are the hurt feelings that result from another's steamrolling. This is basically injured pride—a malady primarily of Feeling people. Patience and endurance of mistreatment are not synonymous with lack of anger. The proverbial "cold shoulder" is fueled by simmering, silent resentments.

A few people even boast that they have no tempers, but this is only because they lack the courage to admit when something or someone distresses them. People with low self-esteem suffer most with this type of inner anger. Smoldering resentments, more commonly referred to as bearing grudges, drag a person to almost a complete stop, demolishing self-confidence in their wake.

Unfortunately, many Christians ignorantly regard the endurance of unfair criticism or personal neglect as a high goal of a believer, as though such treatment can be equated with Jesus' suffering or with "humility." Some even permit physical abuse under this guise. Sorry! Such grievances are most often by-products of poor communication and lack of self-respect.

Angry feelings cannot be ignored or covered up forever. Leave a splinter in your finger and the skin may heal over it, but annoying pain or perhaps a deep-seated infection will be a constant reminder. If you extract the splinter promptly and gently, the wound may bleed and ache, but healing will come. The resentments resulting from ignored anger work like a cancer, eating away at the roots of stability and causing illness, anxiety, depression, sleeplessness, digestive problems, or serious emotional disorder. Any medical doctor will verify this.

Sometimes the silent sufferer allows hurts to simmer and smolder in destructive resentment until the anger circuit becomes overloaded and finally explodes over some minor mishap in a nerve-shattering bombshell. This can subject both the giver and receiver of the angry tirade to mental and often physical injury.

More often, though, an outwardly benevolent bearer of resentment does himself the most harm. Suicides, one of the most frequent killers of teenagers, are often the result of repressed feelings of rejection—a type of ignored anger warning.

Is Anger Sin?

Many Christians preach that anger is sin. Not so. Uncontrolled anger can *lead* to sin, but anger itself is a reminder—a helper. The Bible says, "In your anger do not sin . . ." (Eph. 4:26). In scanning the Gospels, one will discover that Jesus was angry often. Yet Jesus was totally sinless.

Cecil G. Osborne says in *The Art of Loving Yourself* that anger is not evil. It is a God-instilled survival emotion. All human emotions are divine in origin, given to us for our protection, since God wants us to survive. What *is* evil is the misuse of anger, but we have a right to our feelings nonetheless.

Allowing any feeling to influence us toward evil thoughts and actions is wrong. Mishandled anger is certainly the root of many broken relationships and sinful acts.

Since Jesus experienced anger many times, there is evidently nothing wrong with feeling or acknowledging angry emotions. However, Jesus' anger was always on others' behalf rather than for his own defense, thus revealing his holy character. That's love in action—peacemaking.

When evil, injustice, or hypocrisy confronts us, we must show indignation politely and attempt to change the situation. If we do not, we are taking the line of least resistance, which is contrary to Jesus' example. Righteous anger sends many doctors, teachers, preachers, and other workers to the mission field, where disease, illiteracy, and ignorance limit wholesome living and personal fulfillment.

Compassionate anger pushes others to sacrifice comfort and convenience to teach English and technologies to emerging nations and our own underprivileged citizens. Others endure separation from family, experience, poverty, and risk disease to assist struggling Third World countries to attain productivity and progress.

Anger toward emotional hurts stemming from the lack of communication that results in broken homes and relationships causes other people-oriented workers and myself to dedicate every possible minute to counseling, writing, and speaking.

It is important to note that although Jesus advocated forgiveness—turning the other cheek and returning good for evil—he did not sit passively back and allow others to mistreat him or anyone else. Neither did he go out of his way to stir up anger and hostility. In fact, Jesus often slipped away to avoid a potentially hostile encounter— except, of course, when he presented himself as the ultimate, divinely ordained Sacrificial Lamb on our behalf.

Balancing Expectations

Sometimes, in our idealism (and occasionally in our hostility and cynicism), we build up false pictures of other persons and of situations we expect to encounter. Then, if the persons and situations are not what we anticipated, we have problems coping with the unexpected reality. Unfortunately, most people don't know how to benefit from the signs of anger that precede the resentments that inevitably arise when our expectations are unfulfilled.

Marriage break-up often occurs because two immature

people build up false images of each other, as Ethel explains:

> Fred expects me to cook like his mother did. He knew before we got married that I didn't enjoy cooking or being stuck in the kitchen, but he assumed I would change. By the same token, I expected him to accompany me to the opera, which he dislikes. He prefers country-western music and TV football games. We're both disappointed. But since we've learned each other's God-given temperaments, we can forgive the other for not fulfilling our baseless expectations.

When the reality of a mate's humanity is discovered, both partners may be stunned. Similarly, without realizing it, parents often contribute to the unreal images their children have of them. Then, when the children find that their parents have human weaknesses and inabilities, they are disillusioned and feel angry. Resentments sneak in easily in such situations.

Profiting from Anger

Since unsettled hurts emerge as resentment, then expand to bitterness and hostility, and finally grow to hatred, we need to recognize and deal constructively with these obstacles as they arise. None of us is immune to angry feelings or expert at self-control, but it is possible to learn how to express our feelings positively, no matter how Extraverted or Introverted, Intuitive or Sensing, Feeling or Thinking, and Spontaneous or Structured we may be.

If you are a reserved person, learn to identify, accept, and admit openly any angry feelings. Talk aloud to God. Tell him exactly how you feel and/or write out your thoughts in your personal journal. Perhaps you have a

sensitive friend who will gladly listen while you verbalize
your innermost feelings.

If you are prone to speak too heatedly, too quickly and
foolishly, practice delaying your retorts for an hour or two.
Use your adrenaline surge in cleaning, running, exercis-
ing, or something more constructive. Think completely
through your statements before speaking. Talk over your
ideas with God. Write them out or share them with a
trusted friend.

We can see ourselves as we really are by looking at the
way we react to an oversight, a put-down, an accusation,
disagreement, manipulation, or some deed we have done
that no one acknowledges. Remember that crisis reveals
character. As a negative person or experience enters your
life, regard your emotional reaction as a gift from the
Lord. He is ready to polish the particular area that has
been exposed by your responses. Conflict can be a friend
in disguise.

Study your responses and you will see your character
in technicolor. You can then, with God's help, refine and
work on the revealed weak areas.

Anger and Honesty

Sometimes empty conversation can be a means of evad-
ing the real issues. When this occurs, communication is
not genuine but merely gamesmanship. We are wearing
masks and denying anger signals if we cover up the truth
or say one thing when we really mean another.

Theodore Isaac Rubin, M.D., says in *The Angry Book*
that feeling anger is like feeling hunger, loneliness, love,
and fatigue. Angers reveal our personal needs and crossed
values. Ignoring the feeling does nothing to meet the needs
exposed.

Edna lamented, "I'm afraid my husband will ridicule
me if I tell him how I really feel or will regard what I
admit to be my deep feelings as shallow, childish, or fool-

ish. Or even not so. Many times he has said, 'You can't feel that way. That's the stupidest thing I've ever heard!' Statements like this prevent my being totally honest," she sighed. "I fear rejection more than lack of understanding, so I usually say what I think he wants me to say."

When we cover up our real feelings or pretend that things are better than they are, we are playing dangerous emotional games. Learning to maintain our integrity requires considerable effort, which includes listening to our anger.

A Case Study

Gary and Lynda Miller are both Introverted-Feeling people who experience many silent angers but resist or ignore their friendly warnings. Lynda expects Gary to behave and speak the way *she* thinks and acts, implying that hers is the proper, mature, or best way. She innocently assumes a parental role, which makes him feel inferior and less manly. Lynda's public scoldings or put-downs not only embarrass Gary and hurt his feelings but create resentment toward her as well.

Gary is reluctant to admit his hurt to Lynda for fear she will belittle him all over again or rescold him, which would indicate that she doesn't care if he *is* uncomfortable—a subconscious fear of most Feeling people. When Gary does bring up an offense, Lynda reacts by countering with a strong defense of her position. "You shouldn't get hurt feelings when I try to help you," she defends. Parental "you" statements directed to adult mates stir up anger and invite additional resentments.

Lynda resents hearing that she was responsible for hurting Gary. That creates guilt—a common anger warning. Gary is afraid her second put-down will be even worse than the first, so he bottles his hurt and clams up, preferring peace at any cost. Since Lynda responds negatively

to Gary's defensive retreat with her own version of un-
approachable silence, their communication reaches a
stalemate. They are fighting the signals and neither will
break the silence.

Two such Introverts need to decide ahead of time that
the offended one will automatically become the spokes-
person. Waiting until the one who has offended realizes
that the other person is hurting stymies communication.
This plan corresponds with the Scripture in Matthew 18:15:
"If your brother [sister] sins against you, go and show him
his fault, just between the two of you. If he listens to you,
you have won your brother [sister] over."

"I love Gary too much to risk belittling him again,"
Lynda said. "I'll just not say anything critical, whether we
are in public or in private. I'd rather dislike how he's acting or speaking than feel guilty about hurting his feelings.
I'll just learn to tolerate what goes on. That's easier."

Yet, how unfortunate it would be if Lynda completely
ignored Gary's actions or words that distress and embarrass her. Gary benefits greatly from Lynda's opinions, cautions, encouragements, and approval. But he needs to be
assured that Lynda's comments are meant to help rather
than ridicule. It is her timing and wording that need
refinement.

With practice, Lynda can avoid taking offense when
Gary reveals that her comments hurt his feelings. Rather
than defend herself after Gary reacts negatively to her
rebukes, Lynda can acknowledge his angry but honest
feelings regarding her parental attitude by using "I" statements, such as:

"I would never want to hurt you."

"I'm sorry you were embarrassed."

"I regret that I was insensitive to your feelings."

Whether or not Lynda feels guilty—and whether or not
she *is* guilty—this friendly attitude will encourage Gary
to be totally honest, instead of bottling up his angry frus-

trations. A nonaccusatory gentleness will make it possible for Lynda to get in touch with Gary's deepest feelings.

Confrontational episodes can be eliminated completely if Lynda masters the nonoffensive, adult method of expressing her angry feelings of disappointment in Gary's behavior by avoiding accusatory "you" statements and using nonthreatening "I" statements instead:

"I don't agree with you."

"I was embarrassed by your story."

"I don't appreciate your humor."

"I feel uncomfortable when you horse around."

As Gary and Lynda practice substituting adult responses (using "I" statements), their relationship will quickly blossom. In order to maintain an open communication, the Millers must trust each other enough to share their feelings and then consider the other's suggestions. (We will discuss Feeling men in greater detail in chapter 7.)

Dr. Rubin says that to express one's anger reveals respect for the individual in question: "And shows confidence that the relationship is important and strong enough to withstand bumps in the road. It will not come irreparably apart at the first gust of strong feelings. If anything, it will be strengthened as a result of increased understanding. . . ."

Releasing Stored Angers—Grudges

Anger is a sign that we are alive and well; hate is a sign that we are sick and need to be healed, so says Lewis B. Smedes in *Forgive and Forget.*

A grudge represents the unresolved or unexpressed anger we feel toward someone we believe has wronged us. It is the emotional scab we fuss at until it becomes infected, damaging our relationships and possibly our health.

Getting rid of a grudge resembles the operation of spraying for bugs. Definite action has to be taken. But

how? The following checklist has been helpful to many.
Before losing your cool or retreating into silent anger—

1. Acknowledge the problem. Are you sure it was
   intentional?
2. Consider the source. Do you respect the other
   person(s)?
3. Look at the situation from the other person's perspective. Is he or she hurting? Uninformed?
4. Determine the seriousness of the deed, word, or
   slight.
5. Write down the pros and cons of your proposed
   solution.
6. Weigh the benefits of the solution against the risks.
   Might this help the other person? Yourself?
7. Confront the person. Write a letter if dealing with
   an Intuitive. Be brief if dealing with a Thinker. Use
   a soft approach if dealing with a Feeler. Use facts
   and number them when dealing with a Sensing person. Give an Introvert plenty of time to reply, but be
   prepared for an Extravert's prompt verbal response.
8. Remember to use "I" statements so as to be as nonoffensive as possible.

Anger and Forgiveness

We are never so free as when, of our own volition, we
reach back into our past and forgive a person who has
caused us pain and engendered our resentment. Cherished
resentments mature into diseased grudges that stifle
growth and relationships, as Eileen's story illustrates:

> My parents always took us to church. We were never
> allowed to miss anything. It was really boring much of
> the time, too. But after we children all left home, I noticed
> that my parents stopped going to church except for Sun-
> day morning. When I asked my dad about this inconsis-

tency, he said, "We had to be a good example to you then."
This confuses me, and it doesn't seem fair that they made
us go and just pretended to like what they were making
us do.

After acknowledging that her parents had done their
best, just as she was attempting to do with her own children, Eileen was able to forgive her parents for what she
saw as hypocrisy.

To some degree, unforgiving anger is unavoidable because of our common humanity and sinfulness. We can
handle the problem more easily, however, if we recognize
it and deal with it in an honest and open manner. The
only way to heal the pain that will not heal itself is to
forgive the person who hurt you. Forgiving stops the re-
runs of pain. Like Naomi in chapter 5 who released her
mother from childhood resentments by using the empty-
chair method, even a twenty-year-old weight can be lifted
from your emotional shoulders.

Forgiving heals your memory because it changes your
memory's vision. When you release the wrongdoer from
the wrong, you cut a malignant tumor out of your inner
life. You set a prisoner free. When you do, you will discover
that the real prisoner was yourself.

A preacher/writer friend of mine describes forgiveness
as the garbage disposal built into one's spiritual life. We
flush out the resentments by forgiving. If we do not use
this basic spiritual tool, our lives become foul with decay.

Part of the Lord's Prayer says, "Forgive us our sins, for
we also forgive everyone who sins against us . . ." (Luke
11:4). This is often misinterpreted as an implicit threat
that if we are not good to others, God will not be good to
us. Actually, the true picture is that when a person chooses
to hold resentment and closes the door of forgiveness on
the offender, he unconsciously closes the door on himself.
It is not that God is unwilling to forgive the unforgiving,

but that the spiritual condition of the unforgiving is such that they are incapable of receiving forgiveness.

When you no longer need to talk about someone's offense, that is a sign that forgiveness has taken place. It is impossible for most people to forget the actual event (although Intuitives are better at this because they forget facts so easily). A twinge of anger as you recall the circumstances becomes a warning that can both prevent the wrong from happening to you again and initiate some long-overdue forgiveness on your part.

Peacemaking Anger

Admitted and controlled anger is a positive way toward achieving a better relationship to God and others. It can teach, release, refine, and encourage us to peacemaking action. Appreciating and using your angry feelings as God intended can stimulate you to reach out to help a mistreated person, (even if it's yourself), but can also render constructive assistance to the offender.

Spiritual maturity includes choosing what we will allow to visibly upset us, then controlling how we express our feelings to guarantee the greatest benefit to all concerned. The closer we walk with God, the more emotional control we should have—enabling us to gently express our feelings of anger before allowing resentments to take root. Decide at the beginning of the day that you will allow any feelings of anger to catch your attention and teach you something more about yourself. Handling angers constructively and with optimism leads to peacemaking: "But the wisdom that comes from heaven is first of all pure; then peace-loving, considerate, submissive, full of mercy and good fruit, impartial and sincere. Peacemakers who sow in peace raise a harvest of righteousness" (James 3:17–18).

Properly handled anger purges and cleans out our emotional beings. Listen to what Christine learned from slowly, promptly, and positively respecting her anger warnings, thereby resisting resentment and rejection:

> Familiar taunts of "Moby-Dick" and "whale" greeted me as I made my way across the parking lot. Usually, I rail out against such mocking in a rage and blind fury. Today, however, I calmly walked over to the crowd of teenagers and said, "Okay, I know I'm overweight. But how would you like it if you were all by yourself and a group of persons made fun of you? If the tables were turned, I wouldn't do that to you."
>
> The feeling of self-esteem at having stood up for myself was really good. To have gotten that anger out and neither express verbal abuse toward them, nor let it remain inside and fester, was a real relief. One of the teenagers stepped out and said he was sorry and that he thought the whole group should be ashamed. I felt really purged by allowing my anger to be released in a healthy, honest way. The group was helped and so was I.

Spraying with insecticide and weedkiller, although both are strong and offensive-smelling and often leave behind a visible residue, is a vital behind-the-scenes contributor to healthy and lovely flowers. So, too, in our garden of relationships is the end result worth every ounce of effort.

7

"Domineering" Women and "Softhearted" Men —Selective Pruning

If it is possible, as far as it depends on you, live at peace with everyone. Romans 12:18

Describe your mother in one word or phrase," the preacher urged in a Mother's Day message. Jan's eleven-year-old son sitting next to her responded with a spontaneous half-giggle.

"Did you think of something?" Jan whispered expectantly, pleased to know he had been listening.

"Yeah," he nodded quickly without looking up.

"I'd be interested in your description of me, Tim," his mother probed eagerly as she drove the family home. Tim was the youngest of four, the child to whom she felt she had given the most adequate attention. She could use a good compliment, too, considering that no one except the minister had yet mentioned Mother's Day.

"That's all right," he said with a disinterested shrug.

"No, I really want to know what you thought," Jan encouraged, knowing that eleven-year-olds resist sharing in front of siblings. "No one will laugh at you," she assured.

"Honestly, Tim, it would really help me to know how you perceive me."

"Okay," he agreed reluctantly under her pressure. "Nag."

"That's it?" Jan responded in disbelief. She was so shocked that she impulsively let up on the gas. No one else said anything.

"I can't believe what I just heard," she resisted.

"It's true!" Tim reiterated with renewed confidence. "You're always on my case."

A big lump squeezed into Jan's throat. She was silent the rest of the way home, not only startled by his reply, but disappointed and hurt. How could he say a thing like that after all she did for him?

Women especially resent being called a nag or domineering by anyone, and we'll discuss the solution later.

Are You a Nag?

An informal survey reveals different perceptions of what nagging is:

"Nagging is telling me to do what I plan to do anyway," one husband said. ". . . in about two years," he added with a grin.

"Nagging is complaining about my grades and bugging me to do unimportant things," a teenager said.

"Nagging is disagreeing with me," a third person commented.

"Nagging is reminding people of things they would regret if they forgot," an insightful mother explained in her own defense.

"Nagging is when you won't let me forget what I want to forget," her husband countered, then added, "Nagging is you, you, you; do, do, do."

"Nagging is the perception by a person who deems a repetitive request frivolous or inconsequential," a pompous executive defined unhesitatingly.

"Nagging is helping my family stay on schedule and get things finished so they are not embarrassed and others are not inconvenienced with extra responsibilities," a mother of teens explained.

"Nagging is trying to get me to do something I'd prefer not to do, like dressing up or going someplace I don't enjoy—or trying to get me to stop something which I *do* enjoy, like picking my teeth, spitting, belching, or wiping my mouth with my sleeve," an elderly man summarized.

"Nagging is just trying to get people to do what's best for them, like getting enough sleep, eating the right kind of food, getting the proper exercise, wearing a jacket in pneumonia weather," his wife suggested.

With such varied opinions, let's check a dictionary:

Nag: to pester or annoy by constant scolding, complaining, or urging. To torment with anxiety, discomfort, or doubt. To scold, complain, or find fault constantly. To be a continuing source of discomfort, anxiety, or annoyance. A person, *especially a woman,* who nags [italics mine].

Can you believe that? My source happens to be *The American Heritage Dictionary* (a late-sixties edition, obviously).

Some common naggings ascribed to females are:

"You need to fasten your seat belt."

"You should exercise."

"You ought to call/write your mother."

"Clean your room before you leave."

"When are you going to cut the grass?"

"You must take your bath."

"Slow down."

"Turn that music down."

If you'll notice, most of these nagging statements begin with "you" (or the understood "you") and use such war words as *should, ought, must,* and *need.* That is exactly why they are so offensive. So, anyone wanting to eliminate "nagging" from their character analysis, and see action as well, can accomplish both by substituting "I prefer/ wish/ want/ think/ feel" statements.

We are all guilty about nagging someone about something, sometime—like broken records:

Teachers nag students to finish their projects and homework. ("They get paid to nag," a student explained.)

Children nag mothers about "How long till we eat?"

Mothers nag children about cleaning up their room.

Fathers nag family members about turning off the lights.

Bosses nag secretaries to finish reports.

Secretaries nag bosses about returning calls.

Wives nag husbands about fixing things or cutting grass.

Husbands nag wives to hurry up, or stop wasting money.

Parents nag grown-up children about getting married.

Parents nag married children to present grandchildren.

Grandparents nag young people to slow their pace.

Why is it that it is usually a woman who is tagged (sometimes unfairly) with a "nag" label? "I'd rather be accused of caring too much or being overly protective than be called a nag," many women confide. In fact, some women complain about men who are whiney, complaining, or picky. Yes, without a doubt, certain men easily fit the nagging role. However, worry-wart men are called "concerned" or "sensitive." Women with the same tendencies are "nags."

Feeling people (male and female alike), more than Thinking people, have a greater tendency to nag as well as to acquiesce to another's nagging. Consequently, some men are actually more comfortable and feel safer with a woman who takes charge and keeps them reminded about responsibilities.

Many naggers are like Jan, completely unaware of it. Their sense of responsibility, desire for approval, or fear of displeasing someone presses them into the nagging mold by people who depend on them.

"Domineering"—Male or Female?

Many women resent being accused of nagging and also of being "domineering." Are these two offenses the same? Hear the definition from my pre-feminist dictionary: "Domineer: To rule over arbitrarily or arrogantly; tyrannize. To dominate, control, implying superior authority or power. *To be lord and master*" (italics mine).

Interestingly enough, this definition implies that "domineering" is a male attribute, but we can see that *nagging* and *domineering* are closely related, though not synonymous. If you'll compare the two definitions carefully, you'll discover that "to domineer" actually reflects such authoritarian attitudes as:

"Don't ask questions, just do what I say."

"*My* way is the only way."

"I can blow up if I want to, because I'm in charge."

"You're the weak one. I've got all the facts and the money."

"Shut up and listen to how it's going to be!"

All these statements carry a message: "I am stronger and smarter than you, so you have no choice but to submit to my power." Domineering tactics are just as unpopular as nagging and likewise exhibit little concern toward the person being manipulated.

Keep in mind that domineering and nagging are twin affronts to females. Women counterattack by denouncing some males for their fierce tempers, closed minds, and evident disregard for feelings—a stereotyped modern-male macho temperament. Of course, many women resent male counterparts who arrogantly discredit their opinons or abilities and overlook their feelings. However, men are rarely described as domineering, only as decisive and serious executives and bosses or strong leaders in their homes or society. Men who control by domineering are praised for being "in charge," whereas directive women are tagged with the negative "domineering."

Many Feeling people, without appreciating it, are really more secure with stern, austere Thinkers to guide them. Yet, at the same time, they chafe under an immature Thinker's self-centered, cold logic. Feeling people regard domineering as a serious fault, but Thinkers are convinced that nagging is much worse. Nevertheless, I have never heard anyone project that his or her goal in life was to develop either characteristic, although some people manage to be both! Our aim should be to understand and adjust to others, not control them.

Of the many so-called domineering women I have interviewed (many of whom admit the accusation of nagging or domineering is true), none of them considers herself to be domineering by choice. Most domineering behavior is rooted in a perceived need to nag those who procrastinate or who are lazy or undisciplined.

Actually, all temperaments—male and female—have the potential to be either way, given the right situation. In my opinion, disregard or misunderstanding of the power struggles between various personalities—assertive and passive, logical and feeling-oriented, responsible and irresponsible—is a subtle and neglected issue of the feminist movement.

Just as superfluous foliage in a garden must be periodically trimmed to allow for the healthy development of individual plants, certain human traits must be controlled by selective pruning, in the interest of harmonious living. So it is with domination and nagging—both of which must be eliminated because they rob relationships of rapport, growth, and beauty, mainly by blocking creative communication.

In my experience, many men (as well as women) are clamoring to be released—freed to be who they really are. However, we have to find a way to eliminate these negative annoyances without destroying or upsetting the healthy balance of respect, direction, valuable assistance, and helpful reminders that we automatically donate to each other when motivated by love. Unfortunately, irritating excesses will not merely fall away. They must be gently trimmed with understanding and replaced with more positive "adult" responses.

As already established, domestic flower gardens depend on such expert human attention as watering, weeding, and spraying in order to produce a lovely display. Another critical behind-the-scenes step in maintaining beautiful growth is that of pruning. Unless plants are skillfully, tenderly, and regularly shaped, especially when they are young, they will appear shabby in appearance even though they may be very healthy.

Pruning a plant closely parallels what needs to be done with the habits of nagging and domineering. Just a little introspection will reveal that all of us could probably use a bit of pruning in those areas. Or perhaps learning how diplomatically to resist another's nagging and domineering ways and encourage his or her self-pruning might be what you want to learn. Stay tuned for "the rest of the story."

Issues and Answers

Since women seem to bear the greater burden of being labeled "nagging" and "domineering," let us investigate the conditions that can provoke these outbursts. We will concentrate on the primary seedbed—home—and gain insight through several case studies into both the causative elements and possible solutions to the problem.

The Nagging Memory Bank

Tearfully, Jan recounted her problem: "What a terrible Mother's Day I had yesterday," she moaned. "Tim completely ruined it. Could it be true that I'm a nag?" she questioned. "I've tried to be a good mother, but evidently I'm failing miserably. Tim would forget his head if it were not attached. Is it wrong for me to help him remember things?"

"Why not thank Tim for being honest?" I suggested. "Admit that you didn't realize you had become a nag— always on his case. Tell him you really appreciate his drawing your attention to the problem. You might say, 'If there's anything I don't want to be, it's a nag.'

"Then promise him, 'With your cooperation and encouragement, Tim, I'm willing to do whatever it takes to whip this problem, because the last thing I want to do is boss you around. In order to succeed, though, I'll need your help and cooperation. I've put an alarm clock in your room so you can get yourself up, which will keep me from bugging you in the morning. I'll stop hurrying you to breakfast or telling you when to leave for school.' "

I also advised Jan to promise not to nag her son about putting his clothes in the wash and to stop hanging up his clothes and straightening his room. In fact, she was to tell him she would stay out of his room entirely so that she would not be tempted to criticize. Another suggestion was that Jan promise her son to try very hard not to ask about his homework. And she would stop making trips to school with a forgotten gym bag, trumpet, books, or lunch. Finally, Jan was to say to Tim, "If I nag you about anything, please let me know.' "

Jan followed my suggestions. About Friday of that historic week, and after three tardies and a couple of missed lunches, Tim said, "Mom, I really need your help. I just can't remember everything or get everything done. I guess nagging isn't so bad after all."

Because Tim had chosen to depend on his mother's memory and unconsciously expected her to think for him, he had pressed her into the nagging role. Not too surprisingly, he resented her doing the very things he relied on her to do.

In the future, though, Jan needs to let Tim take some lumps for forgetting things. And she should constantly be weaning him away from depending on her to make up for his own irresponsibility. She can avoid the nagging syndrome by making requests rather than commands: "*I would like* your room cleaned up," rather than "*You should* clean up your room."

Jan is like many Structured mothers, who just want the house kept neat and tidy and their children to learn to take care of routine responsibilities. When children fail, are sloppy, disrespectful to others, or lazy, the mother usually feels somehow responsible, so she beefs up the nags.

The principle to remember is "prune while plants are young." Trim your nagging and domineering tendencies before they become full-grown by substituting "I prefer" statements for "You should/ ought/ must/ need" commands.

As you read the following slices-of-life examples of nagging and/or domineering, apply the principles outlined in Jan and Tim's experience—listening, respect, honesty, communication using nonoffensive "I" statements—to see how these situations could have been modified or even completely avoided.

The Self-Appointed Manager

Phil Martin was distraught because his wife wanted a divorce. The Martins had been married for twenty years and their only child was away in college. He could not understand why Grace had left him, because (as far as he knew) everything had always gone well for them. Phil, an ISFP—a delicate but independent *Rose* with a friendly, fun-loving, and generous temperament—was very attractive to Grace, a typical ISTJ—a decisive *Aster* who was very private, serious, and dependable, and whose word was her bond.

Because Phil put off making difficult decisions or getting started on routine duties, Grace gradually assumed more and more responsibility for running the home. She took over the finances to avoid late charges accrued because of Phil's procrastination in check writing. And she detested wasting money! Although she worked full time outside the home, Grace also managed the housework, cooking, marketing, and laundry. She even assisted with the outside maintenance.

It bugged Grace that Phil needed reminders to get the car inspected, snow tires removed, grass cut, and so on. It galled her even more that he let household repairs slide. He preferred to make fun decisions about where they would go on vacation, vehicle and recreation purchases, especially those involving his pickup.

Grace's resentment intensified as Phil always found time to watch TV, nap, play golf, and fish, even though there were jobs to complete, while she allowed herself no personal free time until work was done—which was never. Phil did not volunteer to do much around the house because he knew his wife liked the way she did things. But they never talked about these conflicts because they were both Introverts. Phil also avoided arguments whenever possible.

Rather than nag, Grace silently seethed with anger over Phil's resistance to making difficult decisions and his failure to complete routine duties. She gradually became the typical, but silent, domineering mate. (ISTJs believe that everyone should carry his or her share of the load.)

Her unspoken and unfulfilled expectations produced a huge crop of resentments.

Meanwhile, as Phil acquiesced to Grace's managerial abilities, he became more dependent on her, which made her feel responsible for everything involving his welfare. "I dislike being totally in charge," Grace admitted. "I really wish that Phil would help make major decisions. I keep hoping that he will grow up, but he seems to get more dependent all the time."

The Martins could have avoided their deep-seated problem had they understood their inborn lifestyle preferences. Grace's desire to finish work before play need not have threatened Phil. Rather than taking over responsibilities that her husband shirked, had Grace been willing to allow and expect him to handle the finances the way Spontaneous people like Phil prefer (despite possible late charges) and to refuse to make every decision, he would have been forced to bear his share and would thereby feel better about himself.

Grace eventually decided that since she had a good job, was handling the chores, and making most of the decisions, she could manage without her husband. Yet Phil had no idea how unhappy and disappointed Grace had been. He figured everything was okay because she rarely complained. One good aspect of nagging is that at least the other person hears when everything is not all right.

If either one of these two people had expressed their basic expectations—he for more affection and she for more assistance with decision making—they could have exposed and resolved many of their differences. (This is a typical problem of Introverts.)

The Substitute Parent

Eugene, an ENFJ *Poppy,* creates the climate that demands his wife's control over his "little boy" ways. "Don't forget to get me up for work," Eugene would remind his wife, Frances, an ENFP *Chrysanthemum*. His mother always did!

Frances would call Eugene after she got to work, to make sure he got up in time to open his business. Accepting the responsibility for waking a husband or teen is the first step toward becoming a domineering woman.

Eugene refuses to hang up his clothing or put laundry in the hamper, make the bed (he's the last one out), or clean the tub, rationalizing that he doesn't want to be "bossed around." He defends, "It's not because I want to hurt Frances. I just don't want her to tell me what and when to do things. I regard that as nagging and domineering. I got enough of that direction when I was a kid."

As a Feeling husband, Eugene wants what he does to be noticed and appreciated. If he does something because Frances requested it, the behavior ceases to be his idea and something worthy of praise. "If I hear no mention of what I did, I assume she didn't notice, so I quit," Eugene added. "It's her work, anyway."

As an Extravert, this husband often mentions what he does, but because Frances is angry that he rarely waits on himself or helps her with keeping the house going (as she thinks he should), she withholds praise. Feeling men need constant praise, but Frances doesn't know this.

"Eugene will only fix something after I've yelled about it for several days—maybe weeks," Frances complained. "I usually don't praise him, because I have so much trouble getting him to do what he should do without being told. He's a grown man. I feel that *I* should be complimented on getting him to do it."

Frances has not only become a "nagging mother," but the domineering mate as well. Taking into consideration that many Intuitive men find repairing and doing physical things difficult should help Frances ease up on her expectations.

"When Eugene is offended or feels unappreciated," Frances said, "he punishes me by hiding in his workroom.

He doesn't like to take his licks. He hates to be blamed for any problem. Boy, do I feel like I have a child on my hands!" she exclaimed. "This is more than I bargained for."

Some wives have the attitude that their husbands are their responsibility to teach. However, since they have already been taught by their mothers, a wife's job is to adjust to what already exists.

The Disappointed Enabler

"My husband, Howard [an ESFP *Daisy*], went in business with his brother to breed dogs, even though I was against it," Jana (an ISFJ *Tulip*) shared. "I was against the idea because I know how irresponsible Howard is, but we really needed the income. I hated to invest the little bit of money we had saved, but he promised me that this time he wouldn't disappoint me.

"After a few days, he fell into his old pattern of getting up late for work, so he'd ask me to feed the dogs," Jana said with a heavy sigh. "I didn't like to but I did it, mainly to encourage him and prove that I believed in him.

"Then he'd forget to pick up the dog food, so I'd do that, too, and later was forced into taking the dogs to the vet and on and on. It wasn't easy with a two-year-old and being five months' pregnant. I didn't complain for a good while because I didn't want to be a nag like my mother and his mother were. But when I realized that Howard considered it *my* responsibility to take care of the dogs every day—not our agreement at all—I really let loose and complained and yelled at him every day, not that it did any good.

"The dogs were noisy and scrappy, and taking care of them was clearly Howard's project. He knows a lot about dogs. I know nothing. Yet he took all the credit for the good things I did and yelled at me when something wasn't done right.

"When his brother complained about the neglect of the

dogs, Howard blamed me for every problem that they developed. He kept reminding me that he was head of the house and that I was supposed to do what he said. Some head!" she added cynically. "Because we lost a couple of newborn puppies, we lost our part in the business. Naturally, it was all *my* fault.

"I just hate to be Howard's slave. He expects me to fill the gaps of whatever he leaves undone, which does not just involve the dogs. He doesn't pick up his clothes or put his tools away. I have to follow behind him. If I remind him of things, I shouldn't; if I fail to remind him, I should have. I can't win," Jana shrugged.

Wives are wise to tell their mates, "I love you too much to allow you to shirk your responsibilities." Again, honest communication and a refusal to do what is agreed the other will do (except in emergencies) force the dependent mate into adulthood.

The Female Chairperson

"I expect you to make the household financial decisions," Frank (an INFP *Portulaca*) told his bride, Rita.

"I took a hard look at Frank's mother and father and realized why he thought this was right," Rita (an ENFJ *Poppy*) said. "His mother had been the financial head of their home. When she wanted new furniture, she picked it out and had it delivered. When she wanted a freezer, she did the same thing. She carried the money, paid the bills in restaurants, made the phone calls. When the children wanted money to go someplace or for clothes or supplies, they came to her. Frank's father [a Feeling man], was happy for his wife to make those decisions. Made life more simple for him. I think his father was a bit lazy to boot.

"I went to work not because I wanted to get out of doing housework, but because we needed help with bills. What does Frank do after my first month's check but buy a brand-new pickup. On credit, of course. He also bought a big compressor. He wants me to struggle with balancing the checkbook but still wants the freedom to buy fun things. I do not like to be in charge of finances, but if I am, I want a little cooperation from him. What can we do to change this situation? He says I nag him to death and look at life too seriously."

Nagging often develops when two people have different value systems. This couple needs to identify the causes of Rita's nagging and get help to set up a budget. This will begin the process of cutting away the causes of their nagging compromises.

Neglected Wife

"I'll tell you what bothers me about my husband," Loretta (an ISFP *Rose*) said. "First, Larry [an ISTP *Gladiolus*] never looks at me. That drives me up the wall. Makes me feel like I'm not a person that counts. And he's not a firm enough disciplinarian with the children. I get tired of doing it all the time, and because I have to, I start yelling and I can get pretty nasty. I feel like an ogre.

"I try to communicate my feelings and wants, but he just doesn't pick up on them. I think Larry wants me to feel good about myself, but he says really hurtful things to me and even hits me. I feel he has a lot of hurt, anger, and resentment from his childhood, more than he wants to admit, and he takes those feelings out on me.

"I do talk to him like I'm his mother because he forgets everything or does not get the instructions straight when I ask him to do something before I come home from work. When I'm in a hurry, I give commands but don't mean anything by it. He takes it too personally.

"He hates my yelling. He slams doors, punches walls, and breaks things in the house. I've done this recently also, but only because I get so frustrated with him. I can't take much more. If he'd only let me know that I was spe-

cial and take me out sometimes or buy me a present, but
I guess he doesn't think I deserve it."

*This couple has gobs of communication, but it's all neg-
ative. She tells him how she feels, but only in a nagging
way, which he rejects. They take turns acting like each
other's parent, then like children. Marriage is for adults
only.*

What Makes a Woman Domineering?

In my experience, a softhearted boy or man draws out
the protective nature of a woman. And, since it is usually
the woman who stays home (although this is fast changing), it is she who most often goes to bat for a sensitive
son and protects him from taking his lumps from father,
siblings, and friends.

If men—while boys—get used to having female protection, affection, and personal attention, they rather expect
it from their mates. Many wives, "motherly" by nature,
are delighted to continue the TLC (tender-loving-care) and
are attracted to men who want the attention they dis-
pense. Helping someone who appreciates and needs support gives a Feeling person a sense of self-worth. But,
after a while, the wife may feel uneasy when her husband
allows others, including herself, to take advantage of him.
The wife of a tender man may fault him for not standing
up for himself and in the same breath criticize him for
getting into arguments about her own tendency to dominate him.

"I really wish my husband would tell me no sometimes,"
Elaine sighed. "I know I'm not always right, but he just
goes along with whatever I decide since it's understood
that he doesn't intend to make the decisions. He says that
he prefers to do it my way rather than have any hassle.
I am forced to make decisions whether I want to or not.
I've learned how, but I still don't like it. I'd like to lean on

him once in a while. I hate to be the final boss, but someone has to run things, and he won't."

In such a situation, children generally adopt the mother's attitude and are likely to lose respect for their dad when he doesn't project his opinions and insist on bearing the weight of household decision making. However, they may also resent the mother for assuming leadership and unconsciously blame her for their father's passive ways.

Daughters especially seem to resent how much control a mother exhibits over her husband. They assume, just from observations, that the mother is essentially domineering and shoves the father around accordingly. Actually, in most cases, the husband has allowed, even encouraged, the wife to be in charge.

"When the children ask you if they can go someplace or do something, what do you usually say?" is a question I've asked many a husband who has accused his wife of being domineering. Invariably they reply, "I tell them to ask their mother."

"So who has put your wife in charge?" I challenge.

"I get your point," many admit.

These mothers get used to wearing the pants, but down deep resent the fact that the father-figure has reneged on his share of the responsibility—a parental drop-out. The more insecure the wife feels about this, the more inadequate the husband feels, especially if she complains. The more inadequate he feels, the more domineering the woman becomes. Thus the cycle continues, and this is the very heart of many marital break-ups. Often, womanizing and/or alcoholism or drug abuse are by-products of a husband's feelings of inadequacy and fears about his "masculinity."

For her own good, as well as her husband's, the wife of a compliant man must avoid making *his* decisions. She should donate her thoughts and ideas but refrain from assuming responsibility for his agreed-upon areas of responsibility. Statements like "I prefer not to decide," "I feel more comfortable if you handle this," or "I have confidence in your judgment" will tactfully encourage a laid-back mate to use logical decision making. (My book, *Encouragement—A Wife's Special Gift* [Baker Book House, 1979] discusses this critical dimension at length.)

Instead of wanting to rule the world, as some people fear, most "domineering" women just want cooperation, assistance, and appreciation in taking care of dual responsibilities.

Special Problems of Softhearted Men

Although nagging and complaining seem to come naturally to certain Feeling people, the problem seems to be intensified when two Feeling people co-exist. What this may signify is two insecure people trying to lean on each other.

"My wife was looking for someone to lean on, but she had to prop me up in order to lean on me," a Feeling man who understands temperament said. "I discovered," he added, "that if my wife knows that I'm aware of what she expects, she will likely quit nagging." When men understand what it is about them that causes women to become mother-hen–like and domineering, the art of pruning can begin on both sides.

Some Feeling men are intimidated by Thinkers of the same gender, so they resort to picking on the so-called weaker sex. Often they talk tough and macho toward women in order to validate their ability to overpower someone. When a Thinking woman and a Feeling man marry, the insecurity dimension is usually lessened, because a female Thinker feels fairly secure, even without approval. Also, when a Feeling man understands the normalcy of male softheartedness, he may not wrestle as much with feelings of inadequacy.

Softhearted men are indeed designed by God. While

they have special problems if they believe they must prove their masculinity, the world is a warmer and more sensitive place because of them. It is quite clear, though, that domineering women are often a product of the dependency of Feeling men.

Authoritarian Men

In all fairness to women, we must acknowledge that many men do nag and domineer women, wives, teens, children, and other men. Male bosses intimidate secretaries and foremen dog those under them. There are fathers who browbeat and mentally abuse their children and wives. Many honestly have no earthly idea that they are the least guilty of doing so.

Many naggers are logical Thinkers, and they nag with an authoritarian air. Women usually call it griping or growling or hitting the ceiling. The offenders usually rationalize by saying that they just want things right. Remember, Thinkers function very well without harmony or others' approval.

One Thinker said to his wife, "You should know that nagging begets nagging," which was just his way to ra-

tionalize his authoritarian ways. Thinkers often nag and criticize when a Feeling person persists in beating around the bush in making decisions or giving explanations.

Listed below are situations gathered from my experience that illustrate male authoritarianism:

1. The ESTJ husband who constantly nagged his ENFP wife about the messy house and meals that were never served on time. Structured husbands need to remember that Spontaneous-Intuitives generally dislike routine housework and deadlines. ESTJ people also have a tendency to take their families for granted, which is a fertile source for complaints or nagging.

2. The ENTJ husband who nagged his ENFP wife about a dusty piano or rumpled rugs. He would not allow her to put packages on the couch but insisted she take them directly to her bedroom before she hung up her coat. She was never allowed to kick her shoes off in the living room. ENTJs think they are pushing people in the "right direction" but they are often pushing people *around* instead.

3. The ISTJ husband who complained and growled to his ESFJ wife that she let the kids sass her and also allowed them to be too noisy. What he did not realize was that Extraverted-Sensing-Feeling people love conversation and can tolerate a rather high noise level. On the other hand, if she keeps in mind his low tolerance for noise and confusion, he will have less reason to nag and complain.

4. As long as Stewart (An INTP *Delphinium*) can keep Vivian (an ESFJ *Zinnia*) feeling inferior, he will be in control of her. He tears her down constantly. No matter what Vivian cooks, there's something wrong with it, and if she picks out some clothes for Stewart, he won't wear them. Her self-esteem has sagged considerably.

"Stewart uses me for excuses when he doesn't want to go someplace," Vivian explained. "He will say, 'I have to check with my wife; she probably has something planned.' But when he wants to go, he doesn't check with me at all.

What Stewart doesn't want to do, he blames on Vivian," she added.

This type of annoying behavior is a form of domineering. Yet, when Stewart successfully intimidates Vivian, he loses respect for her. Vivian refuses to use the same tactics but does want to stand up for herself. (She is trying to avoid self-pity by learning to use "I" statements.)

When Vivian learns to respect herself, Stewart will begin to respect her also. She does not have to apologize for who or how she is. He lacks respect for her because she has acted "thrilled" to be married to him and intimidated at the same time. He has been domineering her from the pedestal where *she* had placed him. He needs to be dethroned.

Sometimes it is "good ole Mom" who bears the weight of the entire household's complaints. Have you heard children nag mothers? "When are you going to shop, Mom? We've been out of Grape Nuts for weeks. I'm tired of peanut butter sandwiches, too. Can't we get some lunch meat?" Or "Mom, can I please go? Everyone's going, and I need to know right away."

Older teens might nag Spontaneous-Intuitive mothers: "Mom, this house looks like a pig sty. I'll never bring my friends here until it's decent." Or, as Wayne groaned, "Isn't there anything in this house to eat? What kind of a mother are you? I have nothing clean to wear and nothing decent to eat."

Husbands regularly nag their wives, rationalizing that "it's for their own good." The complaints are often about finances: "Honey, the bills are past due. We're going to have to pay late charges. You asked to do the books, remember?"

Many overweight wives have shared that their husbands constantly put them down and ridicule them for excess weight that they have gained over the years. They are reminded over and over that something is full of calories as though they have forgotten. "I'd just like to see what would happen to their bodies after they gave birth to three or four kids," one irate wife declared.

"If he'd just give me a little sympathy and support instead of criticism and a sermon," another said, "I would be able to trim down faster. The more he reminds me that something is fattening, the more I want to eat it," she confessed.

Just as with men, women with alcohol or drug problems will often elicit domineering behavior from friends and family, even little children. Though such nagging may be well-intended, it is usually ineffective.

The solution for all parties in a power struggle lies in open communication, which requires effort and cooperation on everybody's part. Respect and communication are closely linked. Respect garners respect. In addition, if Feeling people will willingly cut away their annoying nagging (and some of the behavior that incites others to nag *them*)—and Thinking people will agree to lop off their intimidating authoritarianism—our garden of relationships, minus all kinds of domineering attitudes, will be free to produce a full harvest.

Though pruning can be painful, we can learn valuable lessons from the care given a flower garden. When we know how we nag, domineer, and annoy others, we will wisely cut away these irritations so that the richest communication and harmony can be realized.

8

Blending Temperaments— Adjusting to the Weather

My purpose is that they may be encouraged in heart and united in love, so that they may have the full riches of complete understanding, in order that they may know the mystery of God, namely, Christ, in whom are hidden all the treasures of wisdom and knowledge. Colossians 2:2–3

One can take this temperament typing too seriously," Myrna declared. "Are we just to overlook someone's bad behavior, verbal slips, selfishness, arrogance, tardiness, slothfulness, stiffness and all the other social blunders, just because we know his or her type has a tendency toward it? Isn't it better, and more simple, for everyone to just try to live by the Golden Rule than to attempt to figure others out or excuse ourselves because of how we are?"

If everyone were honestly interested in trying to emulate Christ, there certainly would be a lot less tension. But hostilities, resentments, and misunderstandings exist, even among people who eagerly long for harmony and unity and try their best to achieve them.

Achieving the Climate of Respect and Self-Esteem

We can't really drastically change anyone's behavior or attitudes, but we can avoid allowing others' preferences from overpowering ours and rendering us ineffective. At the same time, we can show due respect for others, ask for theirs in return, and work together toward mutual understanding and communication.

Just like the plants in a flower garden must adjust to all sorts of erratic weather and temperature changes, our best approach as human beings is to learn all we can about others' and our own temperament and try to wield a positive influence by word, pen, and action.

I believe there is no such thing as incompatibility, but merely lack of understanding. Granted, blending some temperaments is like backing two porcupines together— a close fit that demands fine tuning. Only hermits can avoid interpersonal clashes and adjustment problems, which is probably their main reason for being hermits. Since everyone has been given a portion of all the temperamental preferences for physical and mental survival, "blending" of opposite tendencies is not as inconceivable as some might believe.

Both plant and human life are dependent on water, light, and air. All three come in various forms and amounts and are not always pleasant or convenient to use. Sometimes those very elements are taxing or destructive.

To pursue our analogy, let us think of communication as "water," information as "light," and decision making as "air." With a proper mixture, co-existence is possible and growth occurs. However, before these necessary elements can accomplish their task, the "soil" must be sweet and chemically balanced. Applying lime around the roots of a plant will sweeten a sour soil. With humans, proper understanding parallels the contribution of lime by reducing the acidity in a conflict-prone relationship.

Since blending in marriages requires the greatest adjustments, I will rely primarily on spousal examples. Due to limited space, we will consider only the most difficult blends. If you read between the lines, you can apply these same principles to relationships involving employee/employer, parent/child, pastor/parishioner, customer/clerk, siblings, in-laws, co-workers, neighbors, and so on.

Blending Extraversion with Introversion

ESTJ (Geranium) *Husband and*
INFP (Portulaca) *Wife*

"I never knew that turning on the radio as soon as we got in the car irritated Georgia so much," Greg declared. "I would never have continued. Nor would I have talked on and on about nothing, had I known I was violating Georgia's need for privacy. I also feel terrible to think back about how I exploded every time someone pulled out in front of me. My temper was close to the surface, and I ranted and raved so easily with no idea what I was doing to her. How she put up with me, I'll never know!" he sighed, as he looked in her direction.

"Believe me, it *has* been tough," Georgia said quietly. "I just figured there was something wrong with me, because nearly everyone I know talks a lot. There were many times, though, when a headache saved me from accompanying Greg someplace. It was my way of avoiding an unpleasant situation. I guess I prefer headaches to burning anger and a feeling of inferiority," she laughed lightly. "That's probably why my headaches came in the first place," she analyzed. "My doctor often said they were caused by nerves.

"My only quiet time is after Greg goes to bed. He always criticizes me for staying up so late, especially because then

I can't get up with him in the morning. I realize now that sleeping late was another ploy to avoid his constant—not always pleasant—chatter. He is also less likely to turn on the radio or TV if I am still in bed.

"His talking is one reason I create excuses not to go places with him, too," Georgia confessed. "He not only talks non-stop at a party, but he's loud and tries to drag me into his conversation. I just don't like to talk, and drawing attention to me just makes me feel all the more inferior," she continued.

"Now that I know Georgia doesn't like so much conversation, I can cut down on my endless comments," Greg volunteered.

"I would also like to be allowed to finish my sentences— another reason I say very little," Georgia interrupted.

"That's true," Greg admitted. "Since I assumed I was helping things move along, I never dreamed I was creating resentment. I am really sorry for being so crass and aggressive," Greg said sincerely. "I do hope you will forgive me, Georgia, and give me another opportunity to prove that I can be sensitive to your introversion."

ESTJs prefer their language of love to be phrased in verbal appreciation for what they have built, painted, fixed, bought, and so on. They do not necessarily require being *told* that they are wonderful, since they also respond to touch.

INFPs have a unique preference for personal gifts and tender romantic notes, with few words and minimal touch. They hate to be expected to talk, touch, and perform on cue.

After this dose of sweetening—and a climate change— Greg and Georgia's relationship will blossom in the light of the information they have shared, automatically improving communication.

Blending Introverts

ISFP (Rose) *Husband and ISFJ* (Tulip) *Wife*

"We've had two weeks of silence," Sidney confessed. "So you could say we've had no communication."

Obviously, a two-week silence is evidence of seriously disturbed communication, which always devastates a relationship. Silence is a childish technique, a form of anger to show that one is hurt.

"Sidney is not completely innocent," Sonya said. "The reason I am silent is to avoid saying what I know I'll regret. After he demeans my family, and insults me, I have nothing to say to him. That's why I go to bed early, alone."

"I never know what she's thinking because she doesn't ever tell me," Sidney explained. "Some nights I just stay in front of the TV, not knowing if she has gone to bed or if she will be coming to sit with me. On many lonesome

nights I say to myself, 'I might as well go play poker somewhere; she's mad at me.' "

Introverted spouses profit from incorporating a ten-min-
ute "clear the air" time each evening before retiring. Honest sharing about the good and bad from the day is
guaranteed to generate some discussion and release tensions that are certain to gather momentum—and turn
sour—if left untouched. Since neither likes to go first,
"alternating" is the first rule of the game. With each talking for an uninterrupted span of no longer than five minutes, the communication process will become easier with
practice.

If either has shared a grievance against the other, the
listening mate may want to preface any defensive comments with "I hear you saying. . . ." Repeating what you
think you heard assures the injured party that he or she
has been understood, and misinterpretation is often the
main obstacle to overcome in a disagreement. Some couples call this time their "dumping grounds," but the practice is wisely suggested in Ephesians 4:26: ". . . . Do not
let the sun go down while you are still angry. . . ."

Two Introverts like Sidney and Sonya tend to expect
the worst to happen and may be pessimistic about many
things. Being around other people may tire them, but feeling decision makers need people to be brought into their
lives to some extent, although the reasons for doing this
will differ. ISFJs (like Sonya) want to serve and host,
whereas ISFPs (like Sidney) prefer fun and physical action
with other people (without much talk).

This couple needs air, but making decisions based on
cold, hard logic is this combination's hardest assignment—since neither prefers a Thinking approach. They
will need to encourage each other to consult logic, but may
experience a strong tugging at their heartstrings when
making decisions that are "best," even though they don't
feel right.

The lifestyle-preference difference—the only one between Sidney and Sonya—will present a significant conflict about *when* to do things and finishing projects. The ISFJ will need to learn to be more flexible; the ISFP will want to be more disciplined and time-conscious. Fortunately, this couple's language of love is similar, both liking practical gifts, and private, physical touching when mixed with genuine, well-chosen expressions.

Blending Intuitives

INTJ (Iris) *Husband and ENFJ* (Poppy) *Wife*

Celeste has enjoyed being at home with the children but is delighted to be back in the swing of the adult world of teaching, where she can exchange ideas, which Extravert-Intuitives usually enjoy most. However, she feels guilty when the housework does not get finished and there is no time to play with the children as she used to.

She also feels guilty because she looks forward to going to work and really hates to go home and face all the homemaking duties. "When men work, they get promotions. When a wife stays home with house and kids, when does she ever get promotions?" Celeste asked. "I want to know that I'm important."

Intuitives must always be making improvements, and recognition and reputation are very important to them. For a woman like Celeste, the main stimulation for cleaning house is to be prepared for unexpected or invited guests.

Ben wants Celeste to work and he likes the added income, but he does not appreciate the fact that she is working two full-time jobs—school and home. He will help her occasionally but feels this is definitely *her* work and is not ready to assume his share of the home responsibility. Celeste feels very strongly that bathing the children, cooking, and cleaning should be equally divided chores.

Celeste is angry and wonders why Ben doesn't give her

attention, approval, and assistance. Though she receives very little positive response from him, he expects her to be ready to make love whenever he wants it. "When I feel unappreciated or that we aren't on good terms," Celeste shared, "I can't enjoy that part of marriage. Ben expects me to turn my feelings off for those few minutes."

Intuitives feel a need to be authentic. "I can't stand to feel like a hypocrite," Celeste confessed. Some wives are happy with gifts or physical services as evidence of a spouse's love and concern. Celeste, true to her type, prefers Ben to say something like "I like your idea," "I appreciate how hard you work, and/or "I'm impressed with the insight and patience you have with the children."

Most INTs like Ben struggle with saying thoughtful things or expressing appreciation or admiration for another's contributions because they don't expect to receive a lot of commendation for what they themselves do. However, they can learn to give strokes, if they have a patient teacher.

Celeste struggles just as hard with making logical decisions and handling mixed emotions. Ben can best help Celeste by not laughing condescendingly at her "emotional" decisions or saying that they are "ridiculous" or "juvenile."

As Intuitives, both Ben and Celeste strive for a flawless marriage and perfect children—an unattainable goal. Ben would want the house to be immaculate at all times. Celeste is more concerned about people—especially their children—than maintaining a perfect house. Because Celeste dislikes disharmony, she will rarely mention her anxieties or defend herself.

This couple's language of love is similar, both preferring the idea of romance to repetitive physical expressions. The ENFJ (Celeste) would prefer that more verbalized compliments accompany physical (private as well as public) demonstrations of affection and commitment, while her

INTJ husband prefers private assurances of respect, with minimal touching.

Blending Sensing-Thinking with Intuitive-Feeling

ISTJ (Aster) *Husband and INFJ* (Camellia) *Wife*

Carol needs approval from Calvin. She has given up a career to care for their preschool children. Keeping the house straight is not as easy as it once was and, even then, it never would satisfy an INFJ like Carol, who thrives on complex assignments.

Calvin works very hard at trying to be outgoing all day long. When he comes home at night and is ready to crash, Carol is ready to cruise. When she mentions how hard she works and how lonesome she is, he becomes very angry because he cannot deliver what she wants—personal time with him.

They argue over the same things day after day. He insists that he is doing his share and just can't give any more. Then Carol wonders if her love for Calvin is slowly dying, and she no longer feels important to him. Carol's self-esteem is at an all-time low because she has eliminated one big source, her career among adults. Though Calvin has not really changed from what he was while she worked, Carol notices his lack of verbal appreciation more since she's so bored and filled with self-pity.

"You mean after I've been politicking all day on my job, I have to push myself some more to give Carol a sense of importance? Having to do any more talking at home just grinds me the wrong way," Calvin muttered. "That's a big order!"

I suggested that giving his wife a bit of verbal encouragement was not an "order" but an investment. "You'll reap great dividends," I explained. "How much is it worth to you to end this bickering? In compromising, you would give more verbal affection than you would normally, and she would expect less than she thinks she needs. Rather than wait until evening, how about giving her attention before you go to work, off the top? Just knowing you are aware of her needs and care about her will go a long way to satisfy her."

ISTJs prefer a language of love that involves having something physically intimate done for them, like having their feet or back rubbed. They also appreciate a spouse who cooks what they enjoy and keeps a house neat, quiet, and orderly. INFJs would appreciate unique personal gifts and romantic notes and less touching. Both types prefer to keep their affection private.

Blending Sensing with Sensing

ESFP (Daisy) Husband and ESFJ (Zinnia) Wife

Sharing the Sensing preference for gathering information through facts and figures seems to make for a good partnership, since spouses who think the same have fewer disagreements, especially if they have other temperamental traits in common, as this couple does. However, this sameness may lead to competition to relieve the boredom, especially after the couple's initial goals have been reached or after the children are old enough not to need close parental supervision. Setting new goals each year offsets this trap.

Coming up with challenging activities will be quite a chore for an ESFP/ESFJ couple, since neither of them prefers the intuitive process, which involves possibility thinking and imagination. Sensing people fall into ruts easily and require lots of information to stimulate their communication.

One way to counteract this is by writing out on slips of

paper various places to eat, numerous things to do, and names of people to visit. Set aside one day or evening of the week to do something together and—if neither has an idea—just draw a slip and do that. Most likely the ESFJ spouse will want to know on Monday what will happen on Friday, whereas the ESFP mate will prefer to decide at the last minute. Deciding on Wednesday would be a good compromise, as would taking turns getting to choose.

Since both ESFJs and ESFPs like to talk, they usually need practice in listening and editing their constant comments. Sensing people also need lots of information to stimulate communication. However, their preferred language of love covers a wide range of experience, both public and private.

Because anticipating future problems does not come naturally for Sensing people, solving relationship conflicts may be difficult for them. They prefer to solve problems as they bump into them—sometimes head-on—leaving them overwhelmed and powerless. In desperation, they may blame each other for being unaware of potential difficulties, especially regarding money and children. Since Intuitives have the ability to imagine and circumvent prospective problems, Sensing people are wise to confide in them and take advantage of their perceptive counsel.

Blending Intuitive-Feeling with Sensing-Feeling

ENFJ (Poppy) *Husband and ISFP* (Rose) *Wife*

Blending these two types mixes an encourager (*Poppy*) with a sympathizer (*Rose*). Like the majority of couples, they differ in at least two temperamental preferences, so they have plenty to work on. But they can be assured that they will not be bored with each other.

When an "idea person" and a "physical-world person"

put their heads together, the result is a clear picture. The Intuitive will think of all the possibilities and the Senser will gather all the black-and-white facts. However, in an argument, they may get no place because they don't really speak the same language. They occupy different arenas. The Intuitive will be wise to write down his or her ideas for the Sensing person to read and consider. Of course, the Intuitive will likely forget some very important facts, which the Sensing person cannot believe is possible. The Intuitive will likely not enjoy taking care of balancing the financial records either, because working with figures is generally a boring chore to this type.

The Sensing partner will be satisfied doing one thing for years, while the Intuitive may show a restlessness from time to time. When a goal is reached, an Intuitive wants to try something new, although that is not always possible.

In our *Poppy/Rose* example, the Sensing-Feeling wife needs to be appreciated for her products and services. Her Intuitive-Feeling spouse prefers recognition for his ideas and contributions in helping people with emotional problems.

Intuitives are likely to draw conclusions and make choices without sufficient factual basis, especially when they feel pressured to make an immediate decision. They hate to admit that they do not know what they are expected to know. On the other hand, being a Feeling decision-maker has benefits as well as drawbacks. Unique problems are created when it is the man who uses his feelings in marital decision making. Since society in general accepts the view that it is somehow not "masculine" to be tenderhearted, a woman is apt to feel insecure with a sensitive man who is easily hurt. Such men often have feelings of inadequacy when they realize that their wives feel insecure.

The lifestyle difference in this couple may cause some friction. The organized, Structured ENFJ will want to plan a schedule, get things done, and work all the time. His Spontaneous, unstructured wife (ISFP) will want to put routine, mundane chores *after* fun jobs and encourage family recreation. The inevitable disagreements will disrupt the harmony they both crave.

Spontaneous people do not like to be pushed. They will react by fighting or fleeing. Spontaneity is not an inferior trait, no matter what Structured people may think. Spontaneous people are survivors and seem to manage having fun despite criticism and others' attempts to schedule them.

A compatible marriage results, despite temperamental differences, when understanding and appreciation are applied daily. Both ENFJs and ISFPs need warmth, affection, approval, attention, and acceptance. The ENFJ will more likely verbalize his needs, while the ISFP will bottle up her hurts and negligences.

Blending Complete Opposites

ENTP (Hibiscus) *Husband and ISFJ* (Tulip) *Wife*

Complete opposites *can* make it! However, until each understands the other's strengths and appreciates the spouse's individual contributions, communication may be rough. The biggest adjustment will be in blending the Spontaneous-Intuitive tendencies of one partner with the Structured-Sensing preferences of the other. The ISFJ will feel that her ENTP husband is constantly springing new ideas and purchases or investing in some get-rich-quick scheme, whereas she prefers long-range, thorough planning based on factual information.

For example, the ENTP may want to take an extended trip but may rebel at the idea of making reservations along the way. Meeting deadlines does not appeal to this type of person. ISFJs usually do not like surprises; they want to be ready for whatever happens. Since ENTPs enjoy excitement, planning things thoroughly destroys that dimension.

Letting physical chores slide (fixing appliances, completing projects, cleaning the car) will without a doubt be a bone of contention for the ISFJ, who prefers to finish one project before beginning another and take care of responsibilities before resting. No one can push or control an ENTP, so the best procedure for this wife is to make "I" statements of what she *prefers* to be done and let it stand at that.

ENTPs freely express their opinions—often controversial—to the dismay and embarrassment of an ISFJ mate, who prefers agreement and harmony. The flip side is that ENTPs are usually very demonstrative with their love and affection and exotic gifts. While ISFJs are a bit more private and practical in showing their love, they acknowledge good intentions and appreciate genuine gestures of caring.

In my experience, ENTP teenagers present the most problems to parents who are Sensing and Structured. ENTPs want freedom—now! They trust themselves, but such parents tend to resist granting freedom until the teen has proven he or she is "responsible." This attitude creates a power struggle. The ENTP is comfortable with relationship risks and seems to be afraid of nothing or no one, which intensifies parental fears.

INTP (Delphinium) *Husband and* ESFJ (Zinnia) *Wife*

Here is another case of total opposites who attract. An INTP is a private, profound Thinker who excels in the field of impersonal design and systems analysis. When paired with an ESFJ—a constant conversationalist who needs warmth, approval, and people all the time—concentrated attention is required to develop and maintain creative communication. This relationship parallels that of the ENTP/ISFJ in the previous example, but learning to blend will produce a very solid, broad, and warm, companionship.

Obviously, an ESFJ wife's effervescence would get on an INTP husband's nerves as much as his solitary independence would be a mystery to her. As long as each considers her capacity for people and his privacy needs, this difference can be handled.

With his Intuitive abilities and her Sensing, fact finding for this couple is at its best. Acknowledging who has the best input for a specific decision is half the battle. An INTP would be better at solving crisis problems, whereas an ESFJ might shine when confronted with dilemmas involving the immediate physical world. Such partners sometimes assume the other person is trying to be difficult, just to make waves, rather than being totally honest in airing their perspectives.

The *Zinnia* will likely have hurt feelings unless the *Delphinium* discovers his ability to modify his generally critical opinions and assures his partner that she is not the object under attack. On the other hand, the ESFJ wife is wise to run her facts through the INTP's Thinking apparatus before making decisions. An INTP would keep his ESFJ wife from being walked on, because his logical approach makes his decisions protective in nature. By the same token, her Sensing powers would keep his Intuitive feet on the ground, because using one's senses gathers information that is closer to the real world.

Any INTP needs to work at being warm, caring, and considerate, as well as trying to be a little more structured. This compromise is an adjustment to both the ESFJ's desire for feedback and her need to know beforehand when and where something will happen.

On her part, the ESFJ wife must learn to taper off her conversation and build up a tolerance for criticism. She also needs to work consciously toward releasing the INTP from an overload of people-business and family frivolity.

An INTP may be more competitive than an ESFJ appreciates. When an INTP remembers that an ESFJ has to have harmony and highly dislikes argument, great strides will be made toward blending these two types.

An INTP's language of love would be expressed in doing something very creatively and quietly, yet spontaneously. This husband would dislike being expected to do or be a certain way or according to tradition. A hug from an INTP is a treasured experience, whereas an ESFJ likes to be touched, talked to, and given presents and compliments. Talk about a challenge!

Total opposites can possess the best of all worlds. When they succeed in achieving a good relationship through the art of creative compromise and skilled communication, they receive the highest honor—The Porcupine Award.

Blending Thinking-Structured with Feeling-Spontaneous

ENTJ (Sunflower) *Husband and* ENFP (Chrysanthemum) *Wife*

Mixing these two types is like blending a catalyst (*Chrysanthemum*) with a head chief (*Sunflower*). Having two preferences in common, like the majority of couples, eases tensions, but their differences in decision-making methods and lifestyle offer plenty of challenge, which these types like and need.

Sharing Extraversion aids communication, and their mutual preference for Intuitive information gathering provides enjoyment and understanding. Both need several goals and prefer a complex life, but friction will likely occur over decision making. ENFPs want approval and people-input before making decisions, while ENTJs make their thoughtful decisions and expect approval afterwards. ENTJs trust their own decisions the most, whereas ENFPs will likely feel steamrolled unless they courageously insist on contributing to final decisions.

Although ENFPs come across as very confident, with feelings of steel, the opposite is true. They are quite sensitive, especially when their ideas or emotions are being ignored or rejected. An ENTJ is wise to slow the process somewhat in order to be gentle, considerate, and verbalize approval and acceptance regularly.

In parenting, an ENTJ will want to be in charge and expect children to obey quickly and remember rules. An ENFP will be less strict or even inconsistent, because this type dislikes rules and schedules for anyone. ENFPs usually do not like humdrum housework or meeting arbitrary deadlines, a tendency that may grate against an ENTJ mate's desire for order. Yet, ENTJs are not usually crazy about taking care of menial, sensory-oriented tasks either.

Although ENTJs prefer to delegate assignments, offering physical assistance greatly encourages ENFPs and can make mundane duties tolerable and more fun. An ENTJ wants to be appreciated for wise, strategic, and practical decisions, in contrast to ENFPs, who want to assist those who struggle with emotional emergencies, giving generously of time, money, and effort (which an ENTJ will deem impractical at times).

This couple's languages of love are very similar. They enjoy unique, romantic experiences and creative gifts, as well as public and private expressions of affection. A *Sunflower/Chrysanthemum* pair can be assured that they will never be bored with each other. ENFPs like to play and have dozens of ideas for activities, especially outdoors. They prefer to gather information at the very last minute, when there is no time left to change it, then make a decision. ENTJs detest indecision and want plans to be firmed up ahead of time so no time or energy is lost.

This particular couple-blend potentially wields much influence in the world because of their natural expertise in openly communicating new ideas with confidence. Their charisma and optimistic leadership also help put their schemes for improvement into practical use.

Blending Intuitive-Spontaneous with Sensing-Structured

Of all the combinations, these types seem to have the most difficulty in relating. Rather than restrict the examples to married couples (and in order to broaden their application), I am including in this section two very common mother/daughter situations. (The principles could apply to father/son, mother/son, father/daughter as well.) When one of the two people is Extraverted, tensions are eased somewhat, but the adjustments are still critical, as the examples reveal.

ENFP (Chrysanthemum) **Married Daughter and** **ISFJ** *(Tulip)* **Mother**

Sue (*Chrysanthemum*) felt like the world was about to cave in, and she expected her mother (*Tulip*) to listen to her problems and offer solutions. When Sue began to relate all the pressures she had—the leaking dishwasher, the dead car battery, her fears about allowing her children to go to camp—Mary, her mother, exploded with "You don't know what problems are. If I had had your problems when I was your age, I would have been happy. If you would get busy and clean your house and take care of the yard, like you're supposed to, and do some cooking for your family, you wouldn't have time to worry about all these little nuisances." (Note that *Tulips* are "servers.")

Sue was hurt, shocked, and disappointed with her Introvert mother's lack of concern. "I'll just not go over there any more," she declared. "If that's the way she feels about me, I can get along without her."

Sue's mother, who thrives on a scheduled lifestyle, feels helpless when her daughter shares her emotional and stressful concerns. The only way Mary knows to handle a crisis is to deny it. She hates unexpected problems.

Mary also feels like a failure because her daughter doesn't like to cook, clean, and sew. "Where did I go wrong?" she wonders. She expects Sue to "grow up" and become adjusted to the real world. If Sue would be like her Sensing-Structured sister, she would get her mother's approval.

ISFJ (Tulip) Daughter and
ENFP (Chrysanthemum) Mother

In this example, the temperament types are the same as in the previous study, though the roles are reversed. This mother/daughter situation illustrates a successful resolution of their conflict through understanding and communication.

"Cindy and I are vastly different personalities," Louise shared. "Before we were aware of this, our personality differences created conflict in our home [Cindy is a teenager]. Now I can appreciate the fact that she likes to receive instructions in steps rather than hearing about the overall outcome that I expect. I also understand why she is overwhelmed with the conversation at our house—the rest of us are all Extravert-Intuitives and Spontaneous at that. Cindy is outnumbered!

I now know about her tendency to worry about insignificant details, too. I can appreciate Cindy's desire to keep things neat and that she wants to know exactly when we are going to leave and return, rather than just jumping up and going, as I prefer.

"We are now able to enjoy each other's uniqueness instead of having it be a source of constant irritation. Since a lot of the friction is gone, we find that we can often laugh over those very differences that used to erupt into arguments. Now that I realize just how special God has created Cindy, she senses less tension and more approval from me. This, in turn, has helped Cindy feel better about herself."

ISFJ (Tulip) *Husband and INFP* (Portulaca) *Wife*

Studies of NFP/SFJ couples reveal common struggles, especially if both are Introverts. After fifteen or twenty years of marriage the NFP sometimes considers leaving, as in the following example.

"For a long time I really believed that I didn't love Roy and didn't want to live with him anymore," Wilma explained. "Now, I know that's not true. I really do love him very much and I want to share this world we've built together."

Wilma and Roy had been married over twenty years and had several adult children. After being cooped up for so long, Wilma craved space. Roy, being a Sensing (and Feeling) person, was on the possessive side. He liked lots of touch and togetherness as a matter of routine.

"When I'd escape to the basement to fold clothes, there he'd be by my side," Wilma complained. "If I was washing dishes, he'd come up from behind and kiss my neck and touch me. This gave me the creeps. He always wanted to go shopping with me and loved to help choose my clothes. I just felt crowded and wanted to be alone. He took all my need for space personally and tried to put guilt trips on me when I wouldn't return touches or verbal affection. It got so that my favorite time of day was when he would leave for work, and my worst moment was when he returned. Yet Roy's a very fine person. I admire him in many ways. Except I just needed space and spontaneity in my life.

"I was so bored with my routine and who I had become that I didn't like *him* either. It seemed like I could do nothing very well. I longed to be somebody. He would tell me I *was* somebody—his wife—but that only angered me. I wanted to be special. Luckily for me and for our marriage, with professional help, Roy learned to back off and not demand my attention or affection. He even learned to withhold what he really wanted to give.

"A lot of Roy's behavior was a reaction to my needing to become 'Wilma,' not just Roy's wife and the kids' mom. I still get really scared when I realize that Roy needs me to be his wife, just as much as I need to be more than that. I don't know how to work that out. I need to be my own person, free to have needs, feelings, opinions, interests, likes, and dislikes. What if my needs infringe on his—and his on mine?

"I'm going to be me, and maybe Roy won't like that person. He said last night, 'If I don't like the new you, I'll pack up and be out like a shot, because I know there's happiness out there for me.' But I'm just too unhappy when I can't be myself.

"Right now I love Roy more than I have ever loved him—but in a whole new way. I'm just beginning to realize how very important he is to me, and I want to spend the rest of my life in the world we've built together. But I won't be happy in that world if it's not okay to be me."

Especially after years of marriage, a Sensing-Structured person interprets marital love as being together at work or play, enjoying their possessions, going places, sharing routine pleasures with children and grandchildren—doing the same things over and over.

Intuitive-Spontaneous spouses expect all of the above in addition to romantic words and actions. Many Intuitives have shared, "I care about my spouse and I don't wish to hurt him [or her], but I have no deep feelings of love anymore. I'm just not fulfilled romantically." Because they are quite bored with repetition, they look for excitement, new ways to pitch woo, and fresh romantic ideas to keep the passion fires glowing.

A Sensing mate is often shocked and astounded to learn that the Intuitive other partner has been bored and unfulfilled romantically for years. Extravert-Intuitives may possibly speak up (or leave) before twenty years, but Introvert-Intuitives just silently hope things will improve.

Riding Out the Storm

How very important it is to know how to adjust to outside influences! Every person we meet leaves a mark and requires some compromise as we interact. In a flower garden, we know that fierce winds and inclement weather force many plants to become stronger and develop a better root system. The elements of nature also clean away ugly debris. So too, can climatic changes improve our garden of human relationships.

The strength of our home life will not only be a strong determinant of our fulfillment as individuals and the quality of our marital commitment over time, but will also dictate to a great degree the self-esteem and well-being of our children and set the tone for the homes they will later establish on their own. For that reason, the next two chapters will concentrate on the marriage relationship in depth. These chapters were written by my brothers, both of whom are experts in the field of marriage counseling and premarital preparation. The material is dedicated to strengthening relationships between husband and wife in a sometimes confusing modern society. The emphasis will be on preventing problems—a favorite challenge for Intuitives—and both Marvin and John have brought their considerable expertise to my work on blending temperaments.

Chapter 9 was written by Chaplain Marvin A. McRoberts, U. S. Army. Better known as Mac, my younger brother first introduced me to the Myers Briggs Temperament Indicator. His thesis is that some of the debris that litters a marriage is nothing more than a collection of myths that are, at best, only partially true and oversimplified. As such, they can disguise the real issues and becloud the underlying love that originally motivated the couple's commitment to each other. Mac debunks some of those myths, thus clearing the debris that stifles communication and impedes growth.

My older brother, the Reverend John E. McRoberts, is pastor of Greene Street United Methodist Church in Piqua, Ohio. John shares in chapter 10 insight from his extensive counseling experiences by outlining the steps he has used to advantage in advising couples who are contemplating marriage and those who are already married but seeking help in achieving a better relationship.

9

The Myths of Marriage—
Clearing the Debris
Chaplain Marvin A. McRoberts

For this reason a man will leave his father and mother and be united to his wife, and they will become one flesh. Genesis 2:24

Most marriages reflect in their various degrees of success or failure the divergent temperaments and expectations that the individual partners carry into their relationships. People bring into their marriages many assumptions that they seldom discuss with their mates. Either they think their spouses share the same expectations or they are themselves unaware of their own assumptions. Since some of these preconceived notions are absorbed from their parents' marriages, many of them remain at least partially buried in the subconscious level.

Other distorted perceptions of marriage are caught from romantic stereotypes in popular love songs, literature, and advertising. Still others are gained from the misguided comments of relatives, peers, Sunday-school teachers, or preachers.

At times, adult children will want for their marriages the opposite of what they observed in their parents' relationship. I have frequently heard a discouraged spouse say, "My marriage is just like my parents', and I thought that could never happen to me." Creating a difference is not easily done, since it usually involves sweeping away some accumulated debris—misconceptions about ourselves and others, and about the "real world."

If we allow for differences among God's people, we are well on the way to building our own self-esteem and properly respecting others. If we also recognize that each marriage involves two unique individuals and pay specific attention to their differences, we are on the right track for achieving greater satisfaction in that union.

Sorting out what is truth and what is fiction in our concept of marriage is a logical beginning point, and that is my intent. Some common myths that my counselees tend to believe about the marriage union have caused them to cling to unreasonable expectations for their marriages. A "myth" is a widely accepted generalization that is not necessarily true. Some myths may indeed have a thread of truth, but they oversimplify the case by ignoring some important factors. Others are totally false. Some of the myths of marriage to be discussed here may apply to your own situation more than others, but you should at least talk with your spouse about which ones may be affecting your union. This list is not exhaustive (you may think of some to add). Neither is it presented in any ranking order of priority.

Debunking the Myths

Myth #1: Biblical Marriages Provide the Best Examples

"The best marriage is a biblical marriage." Few would question that statement, since it implies a truly admirable goal for any Christian couple. One may wonder, however, what is meant by a "biblical" marriage, especially since most scriptural examples of marriages come from the Old Testament and thus pre-date the life-changing events of the gospel story.

Adam and Eve. The first human couple certainly caused their own marital stress! After Eve ate the forbidden fruit, she immediately involved Adam in the act of disobedience against God's command that they not eat from the tree of life: "She also gave some to her husband . . . and he ate it" (Gen. 3:6b). As a result of his behavior (we note that he tried to blame it on his wife!), Adam lost his privileges in the Creator's marvelous garden and henceforth had to earn his living by the sweat of his brow. Eve would experience pain in childbirth for her disobedience to God (and also would be afraid of snakes).

Is this the "biblical" marriage that we should emulate as a model today? Of course not, since believers know that our *first* allegiance must be to God and his commands.

Abraham and Sarah. This couple has long been admired as a perfect twosome. But were they? Though we don't know how they met, we do know how the marriage functioned. Abraham was guilty of questionable and somewhat cowardly behavior as a husband. Because Sarah was beautiful, he asked her to pretend she was his sister. Otherwise, Abraham explained to his wife, "When the Egyptians see you, they will say, 'This is his wife.' Then they will kill me but will let you live" (Gen. 12:12). We know what his primary concern was, don't we? Sarah *was* Abraham's half-sister, but he stretched the truth. Sarah was added to Pharaoh's harem and Abraham was treated well. But God was displeased and sent trouble to Pharaoh, who was riled at Abraham for his duplicity. Although Abraham admitted he had used his wife to protect himself, he did not learn anything from the experience, for he repeated the very same deception after he left Egypt (Gen. 20:1–7). Is this the "biblical" marriage you want to copy—

one in which one partner manipulates the other for selfish reasons?

Isaac and Rebekah. This married pair got off to a terrific start! The Lord was their matchmaker (see Gen. 24). How perfectly they fit the traditional phrase "Whom God has joined together." ". . . she became his wife, and he loved her," the Scripture states (v. 67), but they allowed something to come between them: their children.

Genesis 25:28 describes the problem very simply: "Isaac, who had a taste for wild game, loved Esau [who was a hunter], but Rebekah loved Jacob [a quiet man who stayed at home]." The parents' favoritism toward their sons contaminated their beautiful love story and probably contributed to the children's rivalry and Isaac's scheme to "buy" his brother's birthright.

Years of counseling married couples and families have convinced me that the involvement of children in marital decisions is more common than not. Whether the marriage condition is good or bad, a negative impact on the children is inevitable. Do Isaac and Rebekah represent the kind of marriage you want? Or do you realize that—after God—your spouse's welfare supersedes any other loyalties?

Don't misunderstand my position on "biblical" marriages. The Bible has much to say constructively about our relationships with *all* others, including a spouse. We need nonetheless to clarify what we actually mean when we claim that ours is a Scripture-based relationship. First Corinthians 13 is an excellent measure for those who think they have done everything they can to make their marriage work. Few can stand up to the best standard of love, which includes being "patient" and "kind," not insisting on one's own way, and always protects, trusts, hopes, and endures.

Myth #2: Honeymoons Should Never End

In a good marriage, the honeymoon goes on and on. Or does it? Most folks who have been married just one year

know the honeymoon is over. In fact, some didn't particularly enjoy their actual honeymoon that much. There
were so many adjustments to make that, if given a choice,
they would not want it to continue. But for those of you
who did start your marriage on an emotional high—a romantic encounter that seemed almost heavenly—it is
probably in your best interests to challenge the notion
that implies something is seriously wrong with your marriage if you no longer are experiencing the bliss you felt
as newlyweds.

While working with military families as an Army chaplain, there was an unforgettable Saturday afternoon at
Fort Benning when the doorbell rang and I greeted two
women on my doorstep. The older one was a member of
my chapel congregation, but I did not recognize her companion, who had been brought by her friend for emergency
counseling. In between sobs, which sprang from a heart
surely broken, the young woman related her sad story.
She had been married for a year to a man she was certain
no longer loved her. Before marriage, she told me, they
had run through fields together, hand in hand, and laughing at a world they would conquer together. All that had
changed. The husband now preferred fishing alone to romantic trysts with his wife. She was crushed.

I am not certain I was an effective counselor to this
woman that day. I tried to interpret the reality about human nature in a way she would understand. But she did
not want to hear that we can enjoy romantic intimacy for
only brief periods and then must draw back into ourselves
for a time. We can tolerate joining together intimately for
only short intervals; otherwise we may lose our individuality. Even Jesus periodically drew away from the disci-
ples with whom he had established abiding bonds of love
and deep rapport.

To pick up on Ruth's analogy, plants retain their individuality. If they were all merged into one species, God's

creation would lose much of the beauty he intended. We owe it to ourselves and our mates not to forget who we are.

Eileen, my spouse of over three decades, lost her mother in the early 1960s. Her dad, Bill, is handsome, winsome, and still a widower. Many women have expressed interest in establishing a relationship with Bill, and although he has never proposed to any of them, he has accepted a few dinner invitations. I recently asked Bill why he was never seriously interested in any of these women, who apparently were worthy candidates for a long-term commitment on his part.

"I will tell you, Mac," Bill stated, "they just can't take the place of Bess. She and I would sit contentedly in the living room by the hour and never say a word to each other. All these other women do is yak, yak, yak."

Bill was expressing a valid point about real intimacy. One sign of it is being able to be silent with a loved one and feel no need for conversation, because any issues have been resolved to the satisfaction of both parties.

Running through the fields hand in hand is far different from sitting in peaceful silence in a living room. The first reveals the blush of early romance; the other is more enduring. I do believe that continued romance in marriage is proper and healthy, but it changes in format over time. Writing notes to each other, sending or bringing flowers, and remembering anniversaries and other special events are all wholesome behaviors that enhance a marital relationship. But to believe the myth that we must always feel "romantic" to keep our marriages secure is an unrealistic expectation and a barrier to maintaining an enduring relationship. Those who require passion and excitement to sustain their marriage may later seek these highs with someone else if they cannot find this kind of satisfaction from their spouses. This attitude does not fit the definition of real love as "not self-seeking" (1 Cor. 13:5).

Myth #3: Once Married, a Partner Should Never Change

Do you think you owe it to your spouse to be the same throughout your marriage? And are you disappointed as you wonder whatever happened to the person you married? Creation has always been a process of metamorphosis. What is true for the rest of the natural world holds true for humans as well. Avoiding change is impossible. Life goes on, and we must constantly adjust to the changes around us and within us. As our bodies change physically, we revise some expectations. As our understanding grows, we interpret our history and our present circumstances differently.

Don't we understand our parents more clearly once we become parents ourselves? As adults, most of us reinterpret our parents' behavior as far more appropriate toward us when we were children than we thought at the time. Yet, somehow, despite all this change going on about us, we expect our spouses to stay the same from our wedding day onward. If their words on any subject change or their behavior deviates from what we have grown to expect from them, we protest, "Well, you never said or did that before." It's a "How dare you!" challenge. Mates even apologize for appearing to be "inconsistent" by changing in some way.

Have you ever heard a parent say to a child, "Why don't you grow up!"? The connotation is for them to become adults immediately before our eyes. Another silly order is "Stop acting like a child." How *should* they act but as children? Either statement expects instant change. But, with a spouse, we want no change to occur—except, of course, for a few traits *we* have labelled "undesirable." We are uncomfortable when a mate changes because then we must adjust our patterns of behavior toward him or her. In the TV show "All in the Family," Archie Bunker could no longer tolerate the stress caused by Edith's going through "the change." He finally accepted as fact that he could not stop the process his wife was experiencing, so he commanded, "Edith, I will give you thirty seconds to change!" It's not that easy, Archie, or that fast. When changes occur, our old responses don't get the familiar results.

Because one mate can do much to change a marriage, counseling with only one person can sometimes be as effective as having both persons present. One person can improve a marriage if the main goal is to change one's own self rather than trying to change one's mate. The most likely candidate to bring about a change in the marital relationship is the one most stressed in the marriage. To tell someone not to change is to will that person not to grow. To prevent any living thing in God's creation from growing amounts to a death wish.

Myth #4: Spotting a Good Marriage Is Easy

Often, in counseling sessions, one or both mates say that they wished their marriage was similar to someone else's. However, what is usually being observed of this "other couple" is only what is seen in public. Perhaps it was walking hand in hand, love talk, or candlelight dinners together that was impressive. It should be obvious that the truth about any couple is known only in the privacy of their home. That is why children tend to know how good their parents' marriage is or was. The happiness level of children still at home often reflects how harmonious a marriage their parents are enjoying.

Many couples who demonstrate public affection often have little private intimacy. Somehow they feel safe showing tenderness in public, just as other couples feel more secure arguing in public. They know that in the presence of others they are more on stage and thus able to get harsh words out into the open without the fear of physical attack. We rarely know enough about other marriages to ascertain their real quality, though we often think we do.

Some marital affection in public is appropriate and healthy, when done in good taste, no matter the age of the couple. In fact, an older couple's demonstration of affection seems especially noteworthy, since it symbolizes the enduring quality of their love through time and change. Nevertheless, it is wise to admire as "model marriages" only those you really know and not those you imagine to be good, from brief, public observations.

Myth #5: A Couple Must Remain Married "for the Children's Sake"

The fallacy of this commonly held belief is the implication that the parents' responsibilities are erased when the children have all left home for good. In fact, our job as parents does not end until we reach either senility or death. We continue to model for our children (as few others can do) how to face life in each stage of growth and change. We even model how to be grandparents. How, then, can parents believe a decision about possible separation should be based mainly on whether the children still live at home?

The most important task of parents is to provide a safe, loving home with distinct values that are both taught and practiced. Of course if the mother and father cannot create a secure and somewhat orderly social environment for their children, they may need to consider separating, though only if they have failed in all efforts to correct the chaotic situation. In the long run, having one parent who provides the quality of life children need for proper nurturing is more important than having two parents who— because of their seriously stressed relationship or abusive behavior of one—create the opposite atmosphere. (Even though my own father was absent during most of my childhood, my mother created and maintained a healthy, happy atmosphere for her children. We had little in wealth, but we knew home as a safe place to love and dispute in a normal give-and-take environment.)

When children discern that their unhappy parents are staying together just for them, they often feel guilty. They feel responsible for keeping their parents in a miserable relationship, and few children wish that for their loved ones. Ironically, I have also verified through my counseling sessions the experts' opinion that children may believe they are the *cause* for Mom and Dad not getting along. It is almost impossible for parents to be stressed with each other without somehow putting the children right in the middle of their squabbles. People under pressure are always looking for an outlet, and the children are just too available and vulnerable not to be made a part of the chaos. Since children carry deep wounds when their parents have an unhappy marriage—whether or not they remain together—this in no way implies that divorce can be easily justified, even when it has an on-the-surface appeal as a solution.

I know of a family in which the two daughters got married earlier than they had planned in order to free their mother to leave their alcoholic father, as she had often said she would do "someday." They knew that as long as they were still home, their mother would not leave him. In their minds, Dad was not deserving of someone as fine as their mother. To their surprise, after they married and left home, Mother stayed on with Dad. Apparently, she had either used leaving as an idle threat against him or, when given the opportunity to do so, found she could not. Fortunately, both daughters made good choices in mates and are happy with their own marriages.

Myth #6: Successful Marriages Are Measured by Tenure

Is the success of a marriage measured by its years of endurance? Not always. Perhaps you have read in the obituary column of an elderly person who died and left behind a spouse of fifty or more years of marriage. We usually conclude they must have found the secret of marriage to stay together so long. I believe, however, that the quality of marriage is more important than the quantity of years together. When you can have both high quality and longevity, you have an enviable marriage relationship. But have you known some elderly couples who are obviously unhappy but seem too stubborn to part?

Perhaps I am too confrontive when someone casually comments how many years he or she has been married. My usual teasing response is: "Oh, is that so? How many of those years have you been happy?" This prompts an interesting reply, once the person recovers from my apparent cynicism. "Some of them" or "Every year, month, and day" are two examples. With some people, I tend to think the first answer is more honest than the second.

It is not likely that we will always be happy in a marriage. Most married persons have probably wondered at times how it would be to be single again, although such thoughts usually emerge only during troubled periods. In taking background information on couples entering counseling, I have discovered that two partners may disagree on how many years they have experienced a happy marriage and may not even agree on identifying the happy times. Each mate experiences the same marriage differently.

Would you be offended if your spouse reported fewer happy years of marriage than you lay claim to? Remember, only you can govern your own feelings, so if you have been more happy with your marriage than your mate, take credit for feeling that way. This could mean that you were more tolerant and flexible or that you expected less from the marriage. It does not automatically mean you did poorly as a spouse because your mate decided to be less happy about your relationship. Ultimately, we create our own happiness, since contentment is determined not just by what happens to us, but how we interpret what happens.

Myth #7: My Spouse Is Responsible for My Happiness

"My mate should be able to satisfy all my emotional and relationship needs, and only then can I be happy." What about this expectation? This could be true only if individuals making such a statement did not need other people in their lives. We are far more social than that! Furthermore, to expect any *one* person to supply all our needs is expecting the impossible. Remember the song "You Are My Everything"? This sentiment seems appropriate during romantic times, but it is not a solid stance for healthy marriage. It smacks of unhealthy togetherness that excludes the rest of the world. Christ is "all things" to us on a spiritual level, but no other being can parallel that relationship in the practical realm.

A healthy individual, married or not, must have friends and casual associates with whom to relate in a variety of ways. It is a mistake for couples to give up their friends when they get married unless the old associations threaten the marriage in some way. A far better approach is to keep the fulfilling relationships and also create new friendships that may enhance the marriage. Your marriage partner should satisfy those special needs you want no one else to fulfill, but this is different from expecting him or her to be all things to you at all times. That unrealistic requirement will overload a marriage and perhaps destroy it.

Just as each tender seedling in a garden needs ample room for growth, lest it shrivel and die from overcrowding, so also does each individual in a marriage. No matter how sincere the marital commitment and how compatible the couple, neither the strength of the bonding nor the potential of each partner can be maximized unless there is room

for individual growth. No one better expressed this necessity for spacing than Kahlil Gibran in *The Prophet:*

But let there be spaces in your togetherness,
And let the winds of the heavens dance between you.

Love one another, but make not a bond of love:
Let it rather be a moving sea between the shores of your
    souls.
Fill each other's cup but drink not from one cup.
Give one another of your bread but eat not from the same
    loaf.
Sing and dance together and be joyous, but let each one
    of you be alone.
Even as the strings of a lute are alone though they quiver
    with the same music.

Give your hearts, but not into each other's keeping.
For only the hand of Life can contain your hearts.
And stand together yet not too near together:
For the pillars of the temple stand apart,

And the oak tree and the cypress grow not in each other's shadow.

Myth #8: The Only Kind of Marital Unfaithfulness Is Sexual

Whenever we hear of "unfaithfulness" in marriage we assume a sexual connotation. "Cheating" on a mate seems to mean the same thing. However, those who work with couples hit by infidelity know that seldom is a sexual affair the sole *cause* of a marriage break-up, but is rather a symptom of general breakdown in the relationship. So often the guilty party feels he or she has been driven into such an extreme betrayal by a mate's attitudes and behavior. (Of course, I am in no way shifting the blame from the mate who obtains sex outside the marriage to the one who has remained sexually faithful.)

Unfaithfulness can occur in a variety of ways, not necessarily sexual in nature. A wife, for example, may exclude a husband from her daily life when babies come. She becomes "mother" full-time and forgets to be "wife." Or a husband finds a woman at work appealing because he can converse with her on a more intellectual or comfortable level than he can with his homemaker wife.

Marriage takes constant nurturing. As soon as either mate allows other interests or persons to replace the special place of loyalty the spouse should always hold, unfaithfulness has occurred, even though no sex is involved (yet). People who are faithful to each other on a continuing basis and in the small matters are less likely to face the awful news one day that the mate has preferred another's companionship, whether in or out of bed.

Myth #9: Only Seriously Troubled Couples Seek Professional Advice

"Only the weakest, most troubled married couples go for professional help" is a comment heard too frequently.

You might be sharing this view and certainly have heard said of others: "Their marriage is so bad that they had to go to counseling." The opposite may be closer to the truth, since couples who come for help often do so mainly because they are caring enough about an already-strong marriage to want to make it even better.

Many married couples who could benefit from some professional help are either too proud to go for it, wait too long, or do not believe their relationship is worth saving. I have noticed that those most resistant to counseling at first (they may have been pressured to go by a mate) often become the most enthusiastic in correcting the marital ills. Perhaps their initial resistance indicates a foreknowledge that counseling sessions will be uncomfortable and require work. They may see it as a significant commitment but one too demanding to undertake.

I reassure the couples I counsel that the changes they instigate and the resulting improvements in their marriage will be *their* doing. Although the counselor is part of the process, the real credit goes to the two people who become honest about their feelings and are willing to risk trying new communication patterns and behaviors toward each other.

What about couples who come to counseling just to prove to themselves (and to others) that the marriage is over? "We even went to counseling," they will say, "and that didn't help us." The truth is, they probably never gave counseling a chance and only went a token time or two.

In my present post with the military in Europe, I am often asked to write statements for soldiers or their spouses who have already decided to separate from each other. They need, they say, a recommendation from me that separation is in the best interest of the family, that counseling has failed, and that the government should send the non-military member back to the States. When I tell them counseling is an involved process, and we won't know if it will succeed until they have seriously engaged in it, some get angry at me. I refuse to say it hasn't worked if it hasn't been attempted! Many couples leave each other in anger, but later want to be back together, although the conflict issues are left unresolved. Others attempt counseling optimistically and discover they can work out their differences. Those are the ones who keep me encouraged.

Although successful counseling can occur with just one mate present, it is preferable that both come together or alternately. Having both parties involved can speed up the process of healing the marriage. In single-spouse counseling, one person is called upon to make adjustments and then must wait for the nonparticipating member to react before other interventions are attempted.

Couples frequently think they understand each other fully, but just can't agree on anything. To their surprise, when they are instructed to listen more carefully to their mate, they often discover that they did not really understand the other's temperament and views. When communicating on their own, they may quit the process by either getting upset or silent with each other. But, in the presence of a third party, the counselor, they can go beyond their usual nonproductive pattern of conversing and reach some points of healthy compromise. We can become very defensive and confrontational when dealing directly with our partner, but may accept from strangers what we will not accept from the loved one.

Myth #10: The Church Has No Effect on Marital Stability

Because some couples who are active church members divorce, those outside the fellowship may assume that the church can make little difference in whether a marriage succeeds. I believe the church *does* make a difference! While pastor of a civilian church, I noted that when couples were having difficulty in marriage, one or both of them would often stop coming to church. I was saddened that these people would turn away from church fellowship at a time when it should have meant the most to them.

Eventually, the truth dawned as to why this was happening. Worshiping with another person is a very intimate experience. Think of what we do during worship. We may share a Bible or hymnbook. We say the same words together as we recite the Lord's Prayer or a creed. We sit close to each other and sing together. As we talk of sin and forgiveness, we are reminded how important it is to love God and show his love in our daily lives. There is little we do that is more intimate than worship. Morever, people in the church, because of the strength they receive from God and his people, have resources available to them that people outside the church know nothing about.

Active church membership will not guarantee a marriage's success, but I cannot think of any healthier way to spend our time together. Worshiping in fellowship will have known and unknown impact on all our relationships. Even if there are no marriages in heaven, God certainly cares about how we manage them here on earth. There is no finer opportunity for us to learn about God's will for ourselves and others than in church. There is nothing better than a good marriage and nothing more painful than a bad one, and we have much to do with which kind we are experiencing. We are not helpless victims of our circumstances and therefore can take steps to change our beliefs or behaviors and create a better climate for ourselves and our loved ones. God has great interest in helping us do so, and he works in this, as in all things, through the church family—if we let him.

Other Common Myths

The foregoing does not exhaust the list of false assumptions we carry into our marriages. At a workshop composed of military couples who had a span of marriage

experience ranging from six months to thirty-five years,
I asked the participants to add their own myths to my list.
Here are some of their responses:

1. If I am completely honest with my spouse, the marriage is guaranteed to work.
2. If I forgive my mate for marital transgressions, my mate will love me more.
3. My marriage should be like my parents' marriage.
4. Marriage is incomplete without children.
5. A man has his work to do and a wife has hers, and there should be no overlap of these duties.
6. A good wife will support her husband in everything, regardless of how she thinks or feels.
7. Finances are better managed by the husband.
8. Since husbands are the head of the family, they should not show their feelings when they are upset or depressed.
9. Friendships should be stopped if one mate disapproves of them.
10. One spouse is not responsible for the other's family members.
11. If a husband fulfills his family duties financially, nothing more should be expected of him.
12. Spouses who work all day away from home should be able to do what they want when they come home.
13. The marriage union guarantees that a person will always have someone as a companion.
14. If you are in love with your mate, nothing more is required to ensure a good marriage.

Either discuss these topics or add some more of your own to consider. If you discover areas that hinder your progress in marriage and cannot discuss them to your mutual satisfaction, care enough for each other to air them in the presence of a professional counselor of whom you both approve.

A young husband mentioned that in his extensive reading on marriage, every author indicates how much work a good marriage requires. He seemed somewhat staggered by this revelation, since he was so new at it and had so far to go. I assured him that these authors were correct, but also that God gives us the strength to do whatever is required of us on this earth. Everything he asks us to do is worth it. Few relationships in this life are more challenging than marriage—but there is none other that can bring greater comfort and satisfaction if we clear away the debris.

10

Marriage Counseling— How Does Your Garden Grow?

Rev. John E. McRoberts

There is a time for everything, and a season for every activity under heaven: a time to be born and a time to die, a time to plant and a time to uproot . . . a time to tear down and a time to build, a time to weep and a time to laugh, a time to mourn and a time to dance . . . a time to embrace and a time to refrain . . . a time to be silent and a time to speak, a time to love and a time to hate, a time for war and a time for peace.
Ecclesiastes 3:1–5, 7–8

I have taken on marriage counseling mainly by being an ordained minister to whom, for over thirty years, folks of the church and others in our community have come for help. That they come indicates they are about halfway to finding a solution for their problems. Over the years I have found some techniques that I can place in the hands of those who are planning to be married or who hope to restore some life into a marriage that has begun to wither.

Some Cultivating Tools

Just as a spade, snippers, rake, weeder, and hoe are helpful for cultivating a garden, there are also tools available for cultivating a relationship.

The Spade: Why Do I Love Thee?

When a couple meets with me for premarital or marriage counseling, one of my tools is the "Love List," which acts much like a garden spade in that it digs beneath untilled territory to uncover some previously undiscovered treasure. The purpose is to start on a positive note.

I hand the man and the woman (let's refer to them as "Adam" and "Eve") each a tablet and pencil and ask them to put the date at the top of the page and begin writing down my dictation: "I, Adam [Eve] love you, Eve [Adam], because you are _____." I explain that each is to write down all the reasons why he or she loves the other person. This is to include physical attractions, personality traits, intellectual gifts, social graces, and practical abilities.

(I will later then ask them to number the items they write.) Then I leave the room for five minutes so they may have more privacy.

When I return I ask each to draw a line after the final item, explaining that though the five minutes may not have seemed enough time, it will prove to be enough for our present purposes. (For some, five minutes is too long and is often a sign that this couple may be far from ready to be united in marriage or work on their existing one.)

I then look at the man and say: "Adam, you have two ears. Put one ear in touch with your mind, your thinking, and put the other ear in touch with your heart, your feelings, and listen to Eve as she reads her Love List to you." I usually have the woman read first, since women are usually more open to doing this type of exercise than men.

Here is an actual list read recently by an Eve to an Adam:

handsome	kind	Christ-like
unselfish	sexy	sticks to his guns
athletic	loving	man of integrity
Christian	open	no-nonsense man
thoughtful	funny	loads of character
considerate	smart	priorities are great
hard worker	gentle	acts like a kid (silly)
sacrificial	sincere	makes people feel comfortable
loves kids	serious	loves me a lot
generous		

At the conclusion of the reading, I ask, "Adam, what did you *feel* in your heart?" (Usually some reference to "warm" or "good" is given.) Then I ask, "Adam, what do you *think* about the list? Any surprises?" A discussion usually follows for clarification. Laughter, tears, and even tender touching sometime develop during this exchange.

Then the roles are reversed: "Eve, listen carefully as Adam reads his list and respond with your feelings and thoughts."

Here is the actual list read recently by the Adam of the Eve who compiled the previous list:

sensitive	caring	easy to love
generous	forgiving	common sense
handy	good cook	intelligent
beautiful	shapely	loves God
loves others	loves me	fun to be with
athletic	joyful	wants to be loved

peacemaker	gentle	problem solver
peacemaker	gentle	problem solver
patient	sexy	not hard to please
adorable	kind	mature at times
teachable	strong	homemaker
simple		

Eve then responds to the reading with her feelings and thoughts. A discussion follows, often with beautiful emotion expressed. I then ask, "Why do you suppose I ask you to do this?"

All kinds of opinions are given. The one I chuckle most about is: "Reverend, you are trying to decide whether or not you will perform the wedding ceremony." My response is that if they are determined to be married, I will perform the wedding ceremony, in spite of any doubts I might have, and be ready to help them if times get rough. (We make a verbal contract to that end, and there are those who take advantage of the agreement as much as ten years after the wedding.)

Next I ask what value *they* sense in doing this exercise. They usually find something of worth in what they learn from the project, some couples more than others.

I conclude this exercise by saying that I have found it good for me as an Adam to think about all the reasons why I love my Eve. The discipline keeps me thinking positively about the fine attributes of my spouse. This creates and maintains a positive feeling about her and helps to keep the negative thoughts and feelings in perspective. It is also good for my Eve to hear from me all the reasons why I love her. This encourages her to maintain positive thoughts and feelings about herself. I also stress that all Adams and Eves should be making new, wonderful discoveries about each other as they continue to live and grow as best friends and lovers.

The couple's next project is to add daily to their Love Lists until we meet for the next appointment. (The four additional assignments given at that time are the four tools to be described next.) The couple is then dismissed with a holding of hands in a circle of prayer.

In the next session with Adam and Eve, I have them mark and number the three virtues of the other they cherish most. The Love Lists are then exchanged, with additions and markings noted. A discussion follows. The Love Lists will be filed with subsequent assignments until the couple's first anniversary, when they will be reviewed "for better or for worse." For that, I suggest the intimate setting of a candlelit dinner, perhaps using the candle that was lighted during the wedding ceremony.

I have found this exercise to be very effective both with engaged couples and at an early stage in marriage counseling, even when the married couple's relationship is seriously wounded and filled with hurtful anger and frustration. Any expression of love at that time is like refreshing raindrops on a wilting plant in the heat of a scorching sun.

The Snippers: How Am I Bothered by Thee?

In nearly all relationships there are attitudes and behaviors on the part of one that "bug" the other party. These pet peeves, no matter how trivial-sounding to an outsider, can erode the strength of even the healthiest marriage.

To begin to snip away the stinging power of these marital bugs, I ask the couple in our first session to take home and independently complete the following assignment as dictated: "The attitudes and behaviorisms displayed by Adam [Eve] with which I have difficulty are _____." Each is to make a private listing and bring it to the next session. The promise is made that only one "bug" from each Not-Love List will eventually be selected for eradication. I explain that through a simple problem-solving exercise, the

two biggest "bugs" between them may be snipped off their
lists.

In the second session, after having reinforced the positive through the sharing of the Love Lists, we turn to the
negative—the Not-Love List. I first ask the couple to
trust me in this process, reassuring them that it nearly
always works, and with good humor on both sides.

Then I dictate the following five steps so the couple can
see where we are headed. Each will work on all five steps.

Step One: My Complaint. A complaint is a negative
feeling directed toward a person because an expectation,
known or unknown, has not been met. However, if this
negative feeling is verbalized as such, it will usually beget
a negative expression in return. When dealing with human relationships, two negatives do not equal a positive.
To complain in an attacking manner is something like
stirring up a beehive in the backyard or irritating a hor-
nets' nest in the orchard.

*From each Not-Love List, a complaint will be selected
and transformed into a preference. Read on. . . .*

Step Two: My Preference. "Adam [Eve], I hope you
know how much I love you and how desirous I am for our
marriage to be at its best. I wonder if you are willing to
help me solve the problem I am having with————."

Before Adam and Eve proceed, I hasten to explain that
after all five steps are set before them, each will look at
the Not-Love List, choose the most stinging bug, and
transform that negative feeling into a positive plea for a
helpful solution to the problem.

A typical complaint listed by both Adams and Eves is:
"You never share your problems with me." Each would
then snip this negative comment from the Not-Love List
and translate it into a positive request: "Adam [Eve] I
hope you know how much I love you and how desirous I
am for our marriage to be at its best. I wonder if you are
willing to help me solve the problem I am having with
your not sharing your problems with me."

This moves the process to the next step. . . .

Step Three: The Clarification. "Adam [Eve], please paraphrase what you think you heard me say." I explain that the purpose of "clarification" is to be certain that the issue is understood in the minds of both Adam and Eve.

It is surprising how much difficulty two people can have in clarifying a simple statement. The difficulty is generally rooted in the amount and type of emotion involved in the issue. Sometimes the statement has to be repeated and paraphrased several times until it is rightly understood. Before progressing in the problem-solving process, the type of "bug" eating away at the relationship must be clearly identified and the pertinent emotions understood by both parties.

We continue. . . .

Step Four: Discussing the Requests. Adam and Eve, facing each other, discuss the issue as fully as possible. I encourage them to "empty out" all there is concerning the matter and to do this as positively as they can. Usually the couple exhibits much laughter, some tears, and a little anger through this stage.

Couples sometimes admit they have tried to deal with the issue in the past but have not been able to resolve it. I remind them that this is what we are trying to do now.

We move to the next step, after apparently all has been said that is going to be said. . . .

Step Five: The Agreement. "Eve [Adam], what is it you are asking your spouse to do to help you solve your problem?"

Eve usually requests that Adam begin to share his problems with her, permitting her to understand what his concerns are and even allowing her to help him deal with them. Such an agreement would snip away her initial "complaint." Often a ritual is designed to facilitate the use of the agreement.

I recall the complaint from one Eve that her Adam always interrupted her conversations in group gatherings.

He explained that he was unaware he was doing this or that it bothered her. She assured him that he was and it did! She explained that it was embarrassing for her to be in the middle of a story and to have him interrupt by finishing the story himself, as though she were not intelligent enough to finish what she had begun—or that he thought he could tell it better.

Adam apologized for his behavior and said he was willing to change, but that the change might be difficult since he had been reared in a large family where it was difficult to get a word in edgewise.

The ritual they developed together was for her to tenderly place her "lovely fingers" (as he had described them earlier in his Love List) over his "beautiful lips" (as she had described them earlier in her Love List) whenever she felt it necessary. At a later meeting I asked them how they were getting along. She said, "I don't even have to touch his lips with my fingers anymore. All I have to do is lift my hand and he gets the message."

Dealing with one "bug" from each list seems to be enough to introduce a premarital couple to this problem-solving model. In the early stages of counseling couples already married—where the Not-Love Lists are usually much longer and more painful—one session may not be enough.

As already explained, after the five steps are dictated, I ask both Adam and Eve to choose the most serious problem from his or her list and then help them work through the two selected problems one at a time. For the next two weeks, they are to apply the agreed-upon solutions. At the next session they will share with me and each other on a scale of one to ten the success/failure rating for solving those two particular problems. If the way seems clear, we will attack the next two biggest "bugs" in their marriage, using the same model. After another two weeks, we will check on the progress made with all four problems. If necessary, two more problems in their relationship will be assigned for similar handling. By this time, if not before, this couple has fairly well snipped away some troublesome stingers in their relationship, and growth is occurring.

The Rake: What Do I Expect of Thee?

In marriage counseling I keep hearing one theme from unhappy spouses: "If I had known you were going to expect thus and so from me, I would have never married you in the first place!" To tackle this problem, a third assignment was developed: "Adam and Eve, please look as deeply within yourselves as possible and try to discover the needs that you expect your spouse to meet if harmony and happiness are to bloom in your relationship." I ask the pair to search for expectations in ten areas: (1) sexual; (2) financial; (3) relationship with each other's families; (4) careers; (5) social life, friends; (6) recreational, leisure; (7) children (if applicable); (8) religious, spiritual; (9) free space, private time; and (10) any other area of importance.

The purpose of this assignment is to wield still another cultivating tool. As the couple rakes its soils of discontent together, it loosens and exposes the sharp-edged pebbles that can interfere with healthy growth. Once that is done, the surface can be smoothed and the two can sow the first

seeds of understanding, with more confidence that they will thrive.

The discussion of mutual expectations often becomes the occasion for revealing new ground for understanding and responsibilities and proves to be that proverbial ounce of prevention. Understanding exactly what is expected and learning how to fulfill that expectation are supremely important in developing and maintaining, a relationship and restoring one that is already damaged.

After the Expectation Lists have been shared and discussed, I introduce the couple to the Role Renegotiation Model developed by John J. Sherwood and John C. Glidewell. I have modified this scheme for specific application to the marriage relationship. At this point I will show how it is used in marriage counseling though I also find it helpful in advising couples who are contemplating marriage.

First, I have the estranged couple stand with me at a chalkboard. I draw a box at the top of the board as follows:

The Courtship

| Gathering Information |
| Developing Expectations |

I ask them to share how they first met and to describe their courtship, which usually prompts some smiles as they try to get the story straight. (This might be the first time they have smiled at each other in a long time.)

Then I add a second box:

The Courtship

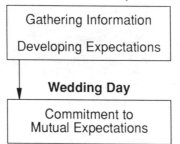

| Gathering Information |
| Developing Expectations |

Wedding Day

| Commitment to |
| Mutual Expectations |

I ask them to tell me about their wedding day and honeymoon. More smiles, perhaps some laughter, and even touching may develop.

Then I add a third box:

The Courtship

Gathering Information

Developing Expectations

Wedding Day

Commitment to
Mutual Expectations

Marriage

Fulfillment of
Mutual Expectations

When I ask for input here, the couple often becomes more serious, even somber. Body language and voice tone may be indications that long-buried disappointments are being exposed.

Then I add a circle: The Pinch.

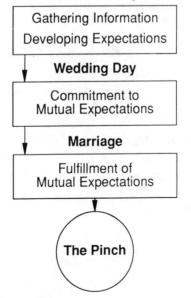

The Courtship

Gathering Information

Developing Expectations

Wedding Day

Commitment to
Mutual Expectations

Marriage

Fulfillment of
Mutual Expectations

The Pinch

The Pinch, I explain, is the fact and/or feeling that an expectation (known or unknown to the other) has not been met. Those "sharp-edged pebbles" can cause pain.

Example: Adam expects Eve to have the evening meal ready by 6:30 P.M., as he thought they had agreed. But Eve begins to serve the meal later and later. The Pinch is felt and a complaint is registered by Adam.

There are three different directions in which Adam and Eve might go in response to this Pinch. The situation is diagramed below:

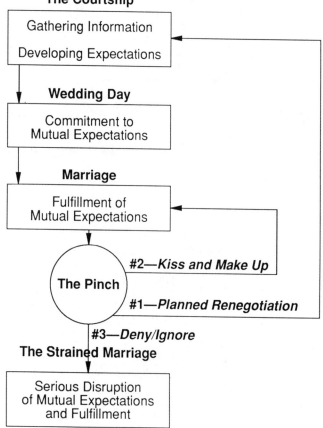

#1. *Planned Negotiation.* This is the best way to handle a Pinch and is outlined in Steps One through Five of "The Snippers." Using our example, Eve may be unaware of how important it is for Adam to have his meal on schedule, or she may feel overly pressured by his expectation. On the other hand, Adam may need to be more flexible and allow for occasional spontaneity. Both will have to consider some compromise on this issue or at least discuss the factors involved.

#2. *Kiss and Make Up.* This is not a long-lasting solution. Eve's apology—"I'm sorry, Adam; I'll try harder"— deals with the symptoms but not with the cause of the problem. It will only temporarily remove the Pinch, even if Adam accepts Eve at her word, since the source of the conflict remains untouched and most likely Eve will "slip" again.

#3. *Deny/Ignore.* The worst way to deal with a Pinch is to deny there is a problem by ignoring its existence. Though there may be no open hostility expressed, the bad feelings of both Adam and Eve will fester until the tension puts a serious strain on the marriage.

At this point in a counseling session, I ask the couple to share with me, if they can recall it, the first Pinch of their marriage and how it was handled. Productive discussion usually follows, but even if some progress is made, we move to consideration of the next circle: The Crunch. This is a big Pinch (or a cluster of Pinches) that is seriously bruising the relationship. I add the four options for dealing with a Crunch to the diagram, which now looks like this:

The diagram now includes the four basic ways to handle a Crunch:

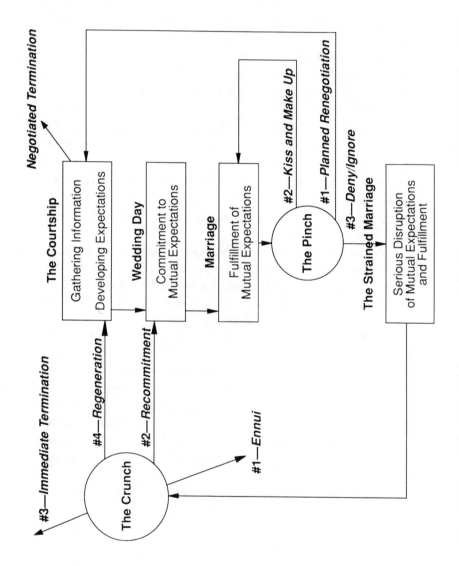

#1. Ennui. Some couples unconsciously choose *ennui,* the French word for "boredom." This attitude of weary dissatisfaction reflects a feeling of being stuck in an unhappy, unfruitful relationship. Long periods of silence and no longer sharing a bedroom may be symptomatic of this condition. For varying reasons, many couples suffer through a counterproductive marriage for months or even years before trying any other kind of resolution. Some choose to live in this state of inertia indefinitely—"until death us do part."

#2. Recommitment. Other couples try to escape a Crunch through a nostalgic desire to return to the past: "Let's start over and go back to the way we were on our wedding day." This rarely works as a permanent solution. It is impossible to recapture a previous time period completely, since circumstances and the individuals have changed since then.

#3. Immediate Termination. Sometimes a couple chooses to terminate the relationship without further attempts to repair the damage. However, a Crunch is usually a bad time to decide upon separation or divorce, especially if it represents the first serious conflict in the marriage. By leaving too many painful stones unturned, there will remain too much potential for long-lasting bitterness.

#4. Renegotiation. The best hope for a marriage lies in confronting a Crunch through renegotiation. The outcome of rethinking mutual expectations in light of what the couple has learned about each other is often the possibility of building the relationship on a new basis of strength. The success of this approach will depend upon thoroughly examining the Love and Not-Love Lists and airing the "complaints" on both sides in light of the five steps suggested in "The Snippers." Sometimes, of course, *Negotiated Termination* is eventually agreed upon as the only way to go. Even so, discussing the underlying problems leaves some potential for reducing the bitterness that has developed in both individuals.

When I hear of a married couple in our church who is considering divorce, I usually attempt intervention. If they agree to meet with me, one of the tools we pick up is this Role Renegotiation Model. My experience over five years has been a success rate of about 50 percent. One-half negotiate to rebuild the relationship and the remainder negotiate to terminate, but it is by far a more satisfactory termination than it would have been otherwise.

In premarital counseling, I present this role Renegotiation Model to the couple and ask them to frame it and hang it on the bedroom wall for future reference.

The Weeder: Where Am I Willing To Go With Thee?

This cultivating tool will help couples plan brighter futures for their marriages and achieve a more lasting, gardenlike relationship. A weeder digs deeply, uproots the nonessentials, and helps the partners focus on the broad quality of life they wish to attain together.

The couple is assigned homework, each to answer: "What I would like our marriage to be like in one year, five years, ten years, and twenty-five years [about where their parents are in life], and fifty years [about where their grandparents are in life]. The question might also be phrased as "How do you want your lifestyle to be like and unlike your parents and grandparents?"

These responses are open-ended and tend to gather up many issues from the expectation lists. It is amazing the various kinds of "life-gardens" each would plan and plant. Next, the couple is asked to create together a "bouquet" from the "flowers" gathered from the "garden" of each.

The Hoe: What Do I Expect to Give to Thee?

Though a hoe may also remove some weeds, it primarily serves to work the soil and make its vital elements more accessible to the plants.

In this assignment I ask Adam and Eve to write a para-
graph that would best say what each is willing to contribute to make the marriage work better. Couples find
such statements comforting and reassuring.

Here is what one Eve wrote to her Adam: "I expect to
be and do everything for you, except those things that
would not be pleasing to God. I am willing to change in
areas to meet your desires and needs as a wife. For example, I don't enjoy eating out, but I will because you love
it."

Adam wrote to Eve: "Dying to self. I am willing to give
time, understanding, patience, unconditional love, effort
and hard work, cooperation, trust, and sacrifice."

After a couple practices using the "cultivating tools" in
counseling sessions, all five assignments are placed in a
folder for safekeeping and referral. A couple not yet married is advised to review all this work on the first wedding
anniversary. Where the reason for seeking counseling has
been concern for the future of an existing marriage, re-
assessment after a shorter interval may be advisable. In
any event, most married couples would profit from a self-
examination of the state of their union, if only as a type
of preventative health care.

Positive feedback gets back to me from time to time.
Here's a sampling: "We were amazed at how much we grew
in our relationship in one year." "We were surprised where
we had slipped during our first year." "We have modified
our goals and what we expect of each other."

The Circles of Intimacy

From an idea suggested by my friend James Faulkner,
I have developed another technique that is sometimes
helpful in counseling, especially for a couple whose mar-

riage relationship has become disarranged for a variety
of reasons. I first draw two circles on the chalkboard:

After explaining to the couple that these circles represent them as separate individuals—male and female—
before they knew each other, I add two more circles beneath the first pair:

This second set symbolizes their affinity when their
lives first touched, when they were initially attracted to
each other. I ask them to share when, where, and how
they met and to describe their feelings at the time. Smiles
usually appear as each tries to get the story straight.
When this happens, I know we are off to a good start.

Then two more circles are drawn on the chalkboard.

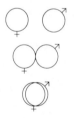

These, I suggest, represent what they felt on their wedding day. The intertwining circles represent their intimacy as newlyweds. Although the degree of intimacy
greatly varies with couples, the key thought is that the
level of intimacy, either desired or attained, was mutually
acceptable on the wedding day.

Each is handed paper and pencil to copy what is on the chalkboard. Then both Adam and Eve are required to add two circles of their own to represent their assessment of the highest degree of intimacy they had ever experienced in their marriage.

Arrangements have varied from ⚭ to ⚭

Next they are asked to date the time of that maximum intimacy and each lists several reasons why he or she believes such intimacy was possible.

After these responses, each is requested to add another pair of circles to represent the degree of their present intimacy.

Eve might draw ⚭ and Adam might draw ○ ○

Obviously the perception of each regarding the present quality of their relationship may be different, so Adam and Eve are instructed to list reasons why his or her model was drawn.

I then ask that one more set of circles be drawn to show the intimacy each desires. Since again the results may vary between them, both husband and wife must write why that particular degree of intimacy is desired and suggest *how* this intimacy may be attained. After the circles and explanations are completed, we begin to work our way through what is possible and what is not.

Such techniques demonstrate that when two people really want to make their marriage grow, blossom, and bear fruit, it will. When one or the other does not want to rebuild the relationship, however, the marriage will continue to wither or dry up and eventually blow away. In either case, I stand by them until a resolution has been reached.

We've Made our Bed, Thee and Me— Let Us Kneel Beside It!

The old adage "The family that prays together, stays together" is more than just a flowery cliché. Paul Tournier has written:

> It is only when a husband and wife pray together before God that they find the secret of true harmony: that the difference in their temperaments, their ideas, and their tastes enriches their home instead of endangering it. There will be no further question of one imposing his will on the other, or of the other giving in for the sake of peace. Instead, they will together seek God's will, which alone will ensure that each will be fully able to develop his personality.... When each of the marriage partners seeks quietly before God to see his own faults, recognizes his sin, and asks forgiveness of the other, marital problems are no more. Each learns to speak the other's language, and to meet him half way, so to speak. Each holds back those harsh little words which one is apt to utter when one is right, but which are said in order to injure. Most of all, a couple rediscovers complete mutual confidence, because, in meditating in prayer together, they learn to become absolutely honest with each other.... This is the price to be paid if partners very different from each other are to combine their gifts instead of setting them against each other.

In the final session of premarital counseling, I offer this advice:

> Adam and Eve, I know you have come to be united in marriage because you feel that your lives can be fulfilled with each other "until death us do part." We have discussed the alarming divorce rate in our society and some of the reasons for this dilemma. I believe one of the ounces of prevention that is worth a pound of cure is prayer. I

want to encourage you to pray together day by day. One of the most beautiful ways I can conceive of this is for you to kneel at your bedside as a re-enactment of your kneeling at the altar while pronounced husband and wife. With your arms around each other, look at each other and inquire how each is feeling about the marriage. Then have your time of prayer together, audibly or silently, and after this—on to bed as "two becoming one flesh."

11

Meeting God's Expectations— Enjoying the Garden

He has showed you, O man, what is good. And what does the LORD require of you? To act justly and to love mercy and to walk humbly with your God. Micah 6:8

Once people discover how wonderfully and intricately they have been created, many just naturally want to praise God, understand his divine purpose, and do his will.

Eloise, after learning how uniquely she had been designed and understanding for the very first time in her twenty-nine years the magnitude of Jesus' loving sacrifice for the salvation of sinners, said it succinctly: "If God did all this for me and loved me when I was so unlovable and not the least interested in him or spiritual things, he must have a will for me. How do I discover it?"

"God's will is outlined in the Scriptures," I told her. "The Bible describes how patiently, lovingly, and consistently the heavenly Father has dealt with mankind throughout the ages. His love will never change, but neither will what he requires of us."

Understanding God's Will

"What does God want me to do?" Eloise probed, as most of us have done at one time or another. Just as parents yearn to hear that question from their child, so God delights to hear it from his children. When we know who we are and *whose* we are, discovering God's will is not such a mystery, since all believers receive insight and instruction from the Scriptures through the work of the Holy Spirit. There are several important truths about himself that God has revealed to us in his Word.

God's Love Is Unconditional and Unearned

The Scriptures state very clearly that every believer is a "somebody" who has been redeemed from sin because of the Creator's love. My personal trek toward healthy self-esteem is directly related to discovering how unconditionally God loves me. If he created me and considers me his treasure, his friend, his co-worker, and his ambassador, how could I ever look down on myself and consider myself a bothersome mistake?

First Peter 1:18–19 declares: "For you know that it was not with perishable things such as silver or gold that you were redeemed from the empty way of life handed down to you from your forefathers, but with the precious blood of Christ, lamb without blemish or defect."

We can never earn God's love no matter how hard we try. The way to please God is by accepting his gift of unconditional love. Though earthly parents may put their children in bondage by setting performance standards, God does not deal with us from such a conditional love base.

God supremely loves everyone—believer and nonbeliever alike. This is very difficult for us finite beings to comprehend. It's sobering (and releasing, too) to understand that God will love you no more after ten years of adult service than he does in your present immaturity as a spiritual infant. There is no way to make points with God.

God's Plan Is All-Wise and Caring

Some people resent and stay angry with God for years or reject him entirely because things have gone *his* way, not theirs. "I'm mad at God," Rene said, "because I expect him to love me through other people. And people treat me lousy," she complained. "It's all God's fault, and he probably doesn't even care."

God does have a plan for each of us, but we have no right to get mad at him because his children misbehave. That's like saying, "Mom, I'm mad at you because my brother hit me."

Rodney was upset with God for not answering his prayers. "I've been working in the post office for fifteen years," he said. "For the last two years, I've not enjoyed my work and I've had stomach pains and headaches. I've asked God to show me what's wrong with me and make me like my job, but he hasn't answered my prayers. I don't think God has any special purpose for my life."

"Maybe, he doesn't like your job either," I suggested. "God always answers our prayers in some way, but you are tuned in for one answer only. You've told him what to do— make you like your job. Perhaps he has another assignment for you."

This INTJ had exhausted the challenge of his hands-on job but blamed his unhappiness on God. Dealing with ill-fitted or worn-out careers or jobs is a common experience, especially for mid-life Intuitives. The problem is sometimes of our own making, and certainly nothing to blame on God. In fact, our very dissatisfaction may be God's way of telling us to get on with what he intended.

God's Way Is All-Powerful but Unfathomable

Questioning God is a popular pastime: "Why doesn't God stop terrorism and war?" "How come God allows innocent people to suffer?" "Why did God let my little girl die?" "Why doesn't God stop drunk drivers?"

"What do you expect God to do?" I might ask the last questioner. "Keep a person from taking a drink or restrain him from getting behind the wheel of an automobile?"

"Yes," most agree. "If he's as powerful as the Bible claims, he could stop unnecessary pain and suffering."

If that's how we expect God to act, we would also have to be willing to find ourselves pushed out of bed on a rainy Sunday morning after a too-late night, being dressed against our will, and forced into a cold automobile to drive to church. Few of us would vote for that! There are restrictions many people request for others but do not want for themselves.

One contemporary writer claims that God is helpless and cannot control events. But my pastor husband says, "God has as much power now as he had when he created this world or designed humans. It's not that he can't manipulate; but God chooses instead not to use the power he has. God won't violate our free will, even when we do terrible things. This ensures that our love toward him is voluntary."

God does not *send* death, destruction, and sorrow, but he may use humanly uncontrollable elements—floods, tornados, droughts, fire—to gain our attention, purify, and strengthen.

". . . in all things God works for the good of those who love him . . ." (Rom. 8:28) is an oft-quoted verse for easing hardship. It does not mean that everything works out for *our* immediate good, but that all events ultimately work together for the good of God's kingdom.

We may not live long enough to witness the long-range benefit of our personal trials, but in faith we can trust

God to unleash our influence and ministry according to his wise plan. Although God has not promised that his power would be used to shield us from hard times, he has promised to help us endure unpleasant and painful experiences.

God's Threefold Expectation

Faithfulness

God first calls us to be faithful—not perfect nor even prestigious and successful. Since he designed us, the Creator certainly knows best how to empower and direct our lives. But, as mentioned earlier, he will not force his will on anyone.

Ephesians 5:2 admonishes: "Be imitators of God, therefore, as dearly loved children, and live a life of love, just as Christ loved us and gave himself up for us as a fragrant offering and sacrifice to God."

Because God is totally faithful to his people, he expects our faithfulness in return. God expects that our right relationship with him will produce a like relationship with our fellowman. Proper worship of God and ethical conduct toward other people are pleasing to our heavenly Father. If we live up to what he expects of us, we can do no less.

Sincerity

God also expects sincerity of spirit, not commercialized religion or a mechanical form of worship. As Jesus implored, "Why do you call me, 'Lord, Lord,' and do not do what I say?" (Luke 6:46).

We need to beware of the temptation to try to manipulate God rather than worship him. It is a faulty assumption to consider what we do in church work as placing God in our debt, so that when we ask him for something he is duty bound to grant it. No one can bargain with God.

Prayerful Obedience

God's third basic requirement has two parts—prayer and obedience—and is recorded in Jesus' words in John 14:14–15: "You may ask me for anything in my name, and I will do it. If you love me, you will obey what I command." Even as we do God's will, he expects us to lay requests before him and allow him to work in our hearts and the hearts of those with whom we have contact.

Since prayer is the most natural product of real love for God, the desire to pray is evidence that Jesus' commandment to love God has taken root and is growing within us. If we do not want to talk with God, can the idea that we love him have any basis in reality? Jesus' death on the cross proved the Father's love and made our communication with God possible.

"In the morning, O LORD, you hear my voice; in the morning I lay my requests before you and wait in expectation" (Ps. 5:3). Until we lay our requests before him regularly, we will not discover the loving companionship he has in mind for us.

Ascertaining God's Will Through Our Strengths

Some very conscientious people assume that God's ideal is to force them to do what is unpleasant or hard, as Yvonne explained by sharing quietly, "We were taught to reach out to people whether we wanted to or not. My minister father constantly reminded us that the Lord—not just our parents—expected this. I was always a disappointment to my dad because I was, and still am, a timid person and find talking to strangers unnatural. Therefore, I've always felt as if I short-changed God. It's like jumping rope for God. Each day the rope gets moved higher—always out of my ability to jump easily."

I have no doubt that Jesus would reply to Yvonne, "I only ask you to come to me and take me as your Savior. Then I can carry your burden and use you for the work I've planned for you, the work that only you can do for me."

God is not unreasonable. He never expects us to do something we cannot do or will not find fulfilling. Our goal should be to get so familiar with God's opinions and his expectations for us that others' opinions and expectations are secondary.

Romans 12:1–2 instructs: ". . . offer your bodies as living sacrifices, holy and pleasing to God—this is your spiritual act of worship. Do not conform any longer to the pattern of this world, but be transformed by the renewing of your mind. Then you will be able to test and approve what God's will is—his good, pleasing and perfect will." We often attempt to limit God through ignorance about our privileged responsibility to discover the abilities and unique gifts of influence and ministry that we can use to inform and encourage others.

Flowers make distinctive contributions besides their physical beauty. Some exude an unusual fragrance that aids pollination by luring honeybees to their nectar. Others produce edible leaves or seeds, useful oils, or herbs for cooking. Still others possess medicinal qualities in their roots or stems. So, too, does each believer have a particular contribution to make in building God's kingdom. Many Christians confuse the terms *talents, fruit of the Spirit* and *spiritual gifts,* but each has its distinctive function, as we will see:

Natural or Developed Talents

An aptitude or skill that one is born with or acquires through training and practice—such as singing, writing, sports, musical ability, dancing, art, crafts, gardening, woodworking—is considered a natural or developed "talent."

In his wisdom and mercy, God has endowed certain people with the raw material to excel and become masters in their fields, like such musical artists as Handel, Beethoven, and Bach, whose works have contributed significantly to both listening pleasure and meaningful worship. In the latter realm, we are equally indebted to disciplined theological scholars who possess the intelligence, insight, and ability to study the Scriptures in their original languages and cultural setting and then provide modern translations for the various world cultures.

Quick analysis of other learned or natural talents would divulge many proofs of God's special enabling and talenting.

Fruit of the Spirit

"But the fruit of the Spirit is love, joy, peace, patience, kindness, goodness, faithfulness, gentleness and self-control . . . (Gal. 5:22–23).

This verse really describes the new nature we receive when we voluntarily give ourselves to Christ. These attitudes develop from our personal relationship with and dependence upon Christ, who *is* this new nature all the time. As believers, then, we have access to all these qualities at any time through prayer. When these characteristics accompany or back up our good works, nonbelievers take notice, are impressed with our demeanor, and are often thereby attracted to our Master.

Spiritual Gifts

Special enablings or abilities are given to believers to accomplish the work of the ministry. As you compare the lists of spiritual gifts given below, keep in mind that all three books cited here—Romans, 1 Corinthians, and

Ephesians—were penned by the apostle Paul, who was no doubt an Intuitive (which probably explains his variation and elaboration of gifts according to his audience or intention.)

Romans 12:6-8	1 Corinthians 12:8-11	Ephesians 4:11
prophesying	wisdom	apostles
serving	knowledge	prophets
teaching	faith	evangelists
encouraging	healing	pastors
contributing	miraculous power	teachers
leadership	prophecy	
showing mercy	distinguishing between spirits	
	speaking in tongues	
	interpreting tongues	

Understanding the Gifts of the Spirit

Source of the Gifts

According to the Scriptures, God bestows the gifts: "There are different kinds of gifts, but the same Spirit. There are different kinds of service, but the same Lord. There are different kinds of working, but the same God works all of them in all men" (1 Cor. 12:4–7). Ephesians 4:7 credits Jesus as the giver: "But to each one of us grace has been given as Christ apportioned it."

God decides the dispersion of spiritual gifts, fitting the gift with the receiver: "All these are the work of one and the same Spirit, and he gives them to each one, just as he determines. . . . But in fact God has arranged the parts in the body, every one of them, just as he wanted them to be" (1 Cor. 12:11, 18).

Every believer has received gifts of the Spirit to be used

for the "common good" (1 Cor. 12:7)—not to be boasted about or admired. Not all the gifts have high visibility or seem particularly attractive, but ". . . those parts of the body that seem to be weaker are indispensable, and the parts that we think are less honorable we treat with special honor. And the parts that are unpresentable are treated with special modesty, while our presentable parts need no special treatment . . ." (1 Cor. 12:22–24).

Most often, our spiritual gifts are in line with what we actually enjoy doing, and these enablings seem to fall along the lines of our temperamental preferences. For instance, most pastors are Intuitive-Feeling people and thus drawn to peacemaking, spiritual ideas, and encouraging others to grow and improve. However, the Holy Spirit often enables a committed believer to use a less-preferred tendency with great expertise when the situation so demands. The Spirit has worked that way in Jim, a rather quiet Extravert-Sensing-Thinker who felt called by God to pastoral service.

As a pastor, Jim is constantly required to consult and use his less-preferred Intuitive and Feeling traits. Though putting sermons together, counseling and ministering to personal needs of a congregation are not easy for Jim, the Holy Spirit has enabled him to develop and use abilities that are "unnatural" for his temperament type. In my opinion, Jim is the finest preacher around, and he has been my pastor for thirty-two years. I might add that Jim's knack for repair and his ability to make logical decisions about financial and physical matters also make him a real asset to a local church.

No doubt we would all agree that asking for gifts is impolite, but we should want them:

> Now you are the body of Christ, and each one of you is a part of it. And in the church God has appointed first of all apostles, second prophets, third teachers, then workers of miracles, also those having gifts of healing,

those able to help others, those with gifts of administration, and those speaking in different kinds of tongues. Are all apostles? Are all prophets? Are all teachers? Do all work miracles? Do all have gifts of healing? Do all speak in tongues? Do all interpret? *But eagerly desire the greater gifts* (1 Cor. 12:27–31, emphasis mine).

Some people erroneously assume that every believer should have all the gifts, using 1 Corinthians 1:7 as a proof text: "Therefore you do not lack any spiritual gift as you eagerly wait for our Lord Jesus Christ to be revealed." This idea throws many conscientious believers into a frenzy of trying to get all the gifts and into feelings of spiritual inferiority for not having a particular gift. But we must remember that God does the calling and the giving. We should not try to impose our idea of ministry on either someone else or ourselves.

A closer study reveals that the promise in 1 Corinthians 12:27–31 is directed to the *entire* church rather than to individuals. It is reasonable to assume that God would not give one person every gift; no one would have time or energy to use them all.

Purpose of the Gifts

There is no doubt that spiritual gifting was meant to equip the saints to build up the local church, the body of believers that Jesus had instituted (1 Cor. 14:12b). Ephesians 4:12–13, 16 explains that the gifts were

> to prepare God's people for works of service, so that the body of Christ may be built up until we all reach unity in the faith and in the knowledge of the Son of God and become mature, attaining to the whole measure of the fullness of Christ. . . . From him the whole body, joined and held together by every supporting ligament, grows and builds itself up in love, as each part does its work.

Spiritual gifts are given to minister to others and accomplish the Lord's work, and they are to be accompanied by the right attitudes:

> Each one should use whatever gift he has received to serve others, faithfully administering God's grace in its various forms. If anyone speaks, he should do it as one speaking the very words of God. If anyone serves, he should do it with the strength God provides, so that in all things God may be praised through Jesus Christ (1 Peter 4:10–11).

First Corinthians 13:1–3 clearly outlines the importance of love:

> If I speak in the tongues of men and of angels, but have not love, I am only a resounding gong or a clanging cymbal. If I have the gift of prophecy and can fathom all mysteries and all knowledge, and if I have a faith that can move mountains, but have not love, I am nothing. If I give all I possess to the poor and surrender my body to the flames, but have not love, I gain nothing.

Discovering Your Gifts of the Spirit

What spiritual gift(s) would you like to have—and why? Our motivation for having a particular gift will probably greatly determine whether God plans to give it to us. The gifts that naturally appeal to us are the ones God usually gives us. Temperament preferences often complement or precede God's special gifting, although *he* makes the decisions about that. We may not feel that we are material for a certain function, but remaining pliable in his hands is the secret for being specially gifted and used. Also, doing something that we are not particularly confident about keeps us more dependent on God.

God often chooses to specially gift those who consider themselves "ordinary," yet who depend on the Lord because they doubt their ability to minister without his guidance. Spiritual gifts of ministry have more to do with one's motivation and recognition of the opportunity to serve than with specific talents or acquired abilities. The Bible gives many instances of such people: Moses, Deborah, Gideon, Peter, Mary Magdalene, and so on. Their special gifting did not really become apparent until they began to work in the Lord's service.

Often, as we are in the process of doing the work of the ministry and need certain abilities, we discover that we already have them. Sometimes others can identify gifts we do not recognize in ourselves. Many people are so aware of their frailties, failures, and inadequacies that they overlook their subtle yet significant contributions.

The important thing to remember is that God decides what an obedient ambassador needs for offering encouragement or meeting another's needs. He also determines the gift's timing. Therefore, one Christian might find that he or she is endued with several unusual enablings during one period of time.

Eighteen years ago, when it became evident that our church needed to provide a children's worship, Jim asked

me to take over the project. I had had training twenty
years before in children's work, but since that time had
been teaching youth and adults—my favorite ages. I was
out of touch with little kids but felt spiritually challenged
and convinced that the Lord wanted me to tackle this responsibility. Many parents were going home after Sunday
school because they couldn't control their children during
the worship service.

No one else seemed as concerned as I was, but I wondered how I would pull this off. I hated the idea of missing
Jim's sermons, singing in the choir, and not participating
in adult worship. Though I really didn't feel excited about
working with children again either, we held children's
worship the next Sunday with our two older children as
assistants.

During those seven years of leading children's worship,
I experienced a special enabling from the Lord. I found I
was able to think on a child's level and write my own
curriculum—(there were no teaching guides then). I received a special spirit of love, concern, and patience for
four-year-olds through sixth grade, as well as the ability
to control an exuberant bunch of kids who had never been
in church. Out of this experience, I was encouraged to
write my first book which was on children's worship, something I never planned on doing. One gift uncovered another.

Many believers have not experienced special gifting because they wait to receive confirmation of a gift before
they begin to serve. On the other hand, some believers
decide that they want a certain gift and stubbornly try to
force God's hand.

When God's co-workers are genuinely committed to
doing his will, figuring out what their gifts are is not that
important. Busy people seem to have more than one gift
and those who have time on their hands seem to have
none, or perhaps just the one that they enjoy for self-
satisfaction.

If we live in the power of God, he will be doing everything he wants to do in our lives. Serious ambassadors for Christ often experience the power of a spiritual gift even before they understand that they are using it. Gifts of the Spirit should be that natural, focusing on the Giver rather than the nature of the gift.

Many pertinent dimensions for the smooth functioning of a modern local church are not found in the traditional descriptions of spiritual gifts. Music, handling electronic equipment, librarian, counseling, keeping the nursery, and just plain listening are a few examples. Since the local church has grown and changed quite a bit since its beginnings, an expanded list of feasible gifting might include:

translating Scriptures	coordination
teaching English	greeters
planning curriculum	financial and other records
writing books/articles	secretarial work
music ministries	telephone work
day-care ministry	visitation of newcomers
inner-city ministry	hospital visitation
assisting handicapped	door knocking/surveys
youth workers	encouraging bereaved
nursery/child care	counseling
building maintenance	bulletin boards
yard care	art work
bus repair	decorating
cooking/cleaning up	jail ministry
construction planning	senior citizens ministry
discipling	

Blending God's Gifts

Keep in mind that any temperament type can do anything he or she is interested in. For example, just because most Sensing people especially enjoy teaching children and senior citizens does not mean that they never enjoy teaching other age groups. And Intuitives, who generally prefer working with older youth and adults, may discover they also enjoy working with children. The same principle applies to "lifestyle" preferences. Many Spontaneous Christians spend endless hours in long meetings without complaining, just as Structured people learn to act quickly in crisis situations.

God calls every type of person to the ministry. The majority of pastors are ENFJ + ENFP but other Feeling types often choose full time church work as well. Although God also calls Thinking types to the ministry, many of them either pastor very large churches, stay at the same church for twenty or thirty years, or migrate to administrative positions within the system.

Relating Typing to God's Will for His Garden

Our research shows that ISFJs, make up the majority of congregations. ISFJs, best known as servers, are good with physical detail and like to get things finished. As members of a congregation, *Tulips* generally prefer to work with either children or senior citizens. ISFJs work without drawing attention to themselves and never ask for compliments, though they appreciate gentle encouragement and quiet recognition. Give them time to respond to facts and think over projected changes.

ISFPs are reserved but quietly independent. *Roses* generally feel more comfortable working with children and senior adults. Though good with details, ISFPs dislike someone breathing down their necks and watching them accomplish tasks. They may prefer to be on a substitute nursery list rather than being scheduled ahead of time.

ISTJs are quite reserved, methodically detailed persons, and often work with finances or physical properties. They like committee work, but they expect meetings to begin and end on time, and are irritated by mistakes. These dependable *Asters* will say what they mean (if Extroverts give them an opportunity to speak). Though ISTJs can teach or preside, they usually dislike being up front.

ISTPs are cool onlookers, alert to external, physical crises involving buildings, buses, and weather conditions. *Gladiola* usually are good with mechanical and building problems (like all Sensing people), but they prefer that excitement and even time pressure be connected with their work.

ESFJs are the conversationalists in a congregation. Since *Zinnias* bubble over with enthusiasm, they make great committee members, coaches, teachers, and planners. ESFJs need harmony and will express what others wish they had the courage to say. They may sometimes volunteer for more than they can handle simply because they hate to say no. ESFJs especially appreciate smiles and verbal praise for what they do.

ESFPs are party lovers, though they dislike cleaning up. *Daisies* enjoy hospitality, are quite entertaining, and will see that everyone is having a good time, whatever work they are doing. ESFPs make fun teachers because they like action and spontaneity. They usually prefer not to be tied down to boring or scheduled jobs but enjoy planning and some committee work.

ESTJs hold together any organization since they are steady, people-persons who will see that programs are carried out, bills paid, floors swept, lights turned off, doors locked, and property taken care of generally. *Geraniums* prefer work with youth or adults. Because they like things to begin and end on time and to run according to plan, ESTJs have an aversion to confusion and wasting time or effort. In short, they want straight answers and like their judgment to be trusted.

ESTPs are talkative persons who handle crises well. They are always in charge when an emergency surfaces. *Hollyhocks* know how to save energy and cut corners and even enjoy a bit of physical or financial risk. Competition turns them on. In their opinion, for example, contests would make increasing Sunday-school enrollment or attendance a fun-filled challenge.

INFJs are quiet observers and problem solvers, but *Camellias* rarely volunteer their opinions or insights and must be asked for their suggestions. They are very unselfish with their time and money, so please don't take advantage of them! INFJs can teach nearly any class that needs a teacher, but they are often very timid about facing a group.

INFPs are very independent, sensitive people who prefer one-on-one confrontations. *Portulacas* are unselfish with their time and money. Their observations are often way ahead of others. Though they are loyal followers, they usually prefer not to lead or to be singled out.

INTJs have the ability to view a situation with singular accuracy. An *Iris* may come across as negative, highly critical, and arrogant, but he or she is a strategist and sees every stone that could be turned. INTJs have the ability to sum up an evening's committee work in a few brief sentences, so they can keep a committee on an effective track. They are excellent consultants. Their teaching is brilliant and usually appeals to adults or older youth. Since INTJs expect a lot from themselves and others and do not like to waste time on nonessentials, they can unwittingly intimidate others.

INTPs are very special people to have in a church organization because of their ability to solve systems problems. *Delphiniums* are usually very quiet and observant and make excellent teachers, though they are easily bored with simple material and have a tendency to teach over the heads of others. If they are challenged to teach children, they will do a fantastic job. They are "possibility thinkers" and would be looking way ahead on behalf of the children. Respect for their ideas and solid judgment pleases them.

ENFJs are liaison people who feel comfortable around almost everyone and are the most diplomatic of types.

ENFJs are great idea people and like to get things done—now. A *Poppy* has a tendency to proceed too fast for most church members but is an especially good committee member. ENFJs insist on harmony and are usually for the underdog. They are natural counselors and chaperones and skilled at working themselves out of jobs and involving others. Appreciate them for their ideas, their desire for understanding, and their genuine concern for group rapport.

ENFPs love discussions and make exciting teachers and leaders. They may not begin or end on time, but the content of what they offer will be well worth the time invested. Usually very popular, *Chrysanthemums'* spontaneity allows them to let church responsibilities drain them of their energy, finances, and time. ENFPs are good in emergencies and love to solve personal emotional crises. Put them to work in jails, detention homes, drug centers, hospitals—wherever people need advice and encouragement. Every committee would be richer by having at least one such catalyst. ENFPs respond to friendliness and appreciation for their ideas and concern for others.

ENTJs are gifted with structured vision. *Sunflowers* see far into the future and can verbally express the design or way to get there. As "head chiefs" they have a real knack for delegating responsibilities. In fact, they may assign everyone a job and then sit down with a cup of coffee and watch things happen. ENTJs are naturals for handling the abstracts of teaching, leading, and committee work. They can deal with heavy responsibility because they do not let their feelings get in the way. Their confidence, optimism, and logical decision making are advantageous in a church relationship, although they often move too fast and with too much complexity for the general public. Trust their judgment and follow their leadership.

ENTPs are the most powerful people-movers. They deal well with crises but dislike long, drawn-out meetings or problems. Like other Spontaneous persons, a *Hibiscus* is very independent. Once a crisis is solved, ENTPs become bored, since they do not like to "oil machinery." Give them complex challenges and watch them work. ENTPs often enjoy speaking and leading conferences and seminars. They seem to do it effortlessly but may not spend much preparation time because they enjoy last-minute, "pull it together" challenges.

Sharing Our Faith

Using our spiritual gifts—leading worship, teaching Bible, equipping workers, helping those who need physical and spiritual assistance—is only part of our responsibilities as Christians. Reaching out to those who do not yet believe is an individual assignment given by God to all believers.

All through the Bible, without respect to type or special gifting from the Holy Spirit, all believers are admonished, commanded, expected, and urged to share the experience they initially had with Jesus and are still having. This involves praising him! Lifestyle evangelism is not a special gift of a chosen few, but is a requirement for every believer.

The Holy Spirit will reveal opportunities for sharing our faith and give the needed enabling. He can empower us for his work, teach us the priority of people, and encourage us as we relate to others in love. Once we understand God's perfect love for each of us and his purpose—to make himself known to the world—it makes good sense to further his intention by using our personalities and abilities to help bring about his kingdom.

Enjoying the Garden

A healthy, beautiful array of blooms, minus weeds, pleases any gardener. In human terms, God is the gardener; you and I are the flowers. Each of us is unique as we reflect upon and influence our neighbor plants and mutually endure changes in the weather, sunless days, and all the enemies a garden shares. We all have potential contributions to make to our immediate neighbors and the rest of the world as we share a common goal: to make the world a better place. Understanding temperaments raises personal self-esteem and improves our appreciation for others, and the resulting harmony among the flowers in our human garden gives God great pleasure.

The essay *The Garden,* by Robert J. Hastings perfectly captures my meaning:

> When GOD created a home for the first man and woman to love and live, he turned his back on marble and stone and oak and cedar. Instead, he formed an Eden of palms and ferns, kissed with dewdrops on daises and raindrops on roses. And to this day, we taste the sweetest love when we find a door that opens wide upon a lovely garden.
>
> Yes, everyone loves a garden, whether a tiny patio where petunias bloom in pots and herbs sprout from window boxes, a farm garden where cabbages mingle with marigolds, or a formal garden on an English hillside, neatly hedged with boxwood and privet.
>
> But favorite of favorites is a garden heavy with the perfume of love. The greens and pastels of spring gardens sing of young and waking love. The lush foliage of summer gardens tells of passionate and pregnant love. The subtle browns and golds of autumn gardens speak of proven love, rich in fabric. And the red berries and shiny evergreens of winter gardens paint a serene and accepting love.
>
> The choicest garden is a shared garden. And so with love, for there is no love apart from shared love. Selfish is the prison-garden that locks within itself the love that's meant for others. Like the tendrils of a growing plant, love reaches out to touch and bless. Like the aroma of honeysuckle, love permeates the hidden corners of lives beyond its own.
>
> Now hear the secret of the garden: It blooms to make

others happy, not to make them good. Likewise with love, for love aims to please the beloved, not to reform. What we can do is to love them through the gates of happiness. And the wonder is that when folks are happy, they are more likely to be good.

This is the secret of the garden . . . this is the miracle of love.[1]

Ephesians 3:16–19 is a wonderful passage with which to conclude such a subject: "I pray that out of his glorious riches he may strengthen you with power through his Spirit in your inner being, so that Christ may dwell in your hearts through faith. And I pray that you, being rooted and established in love, may have power, together with all the saints, to grasp how wide and long and high and deep is the love of Christ, and to know this love that surpasses knowledge—that you may be filled to the measure of all the fullness of God."